RACISM AND CHILD PROTECTION

Also available from Cassell:

R. Best, P. Lang and A. Lichtenberg (eds), *Caring for Children*

R. Millam, *Anti-discriminatory Practice: A Guide for Workers in Childcare and Education*

C. Sharman, W. Cross and D. Vennis, *Observing Children*

B. Singh, *Improving Gender and Ethnic Relations*

V. Varma, *Coping with Unhappy Children*

RACISM AND CHILD PROTECTION
The Black Experience of Child Sexual Abuse

Valerie Jackson

CASSELL

Cassell
Wellington House
125 Strand
London WC2R 0BB

127 West 24th Street
New York
NY 10011

First published 1996

British Library Cataloguing-in-Publication Data
A catalogue record for this book is available from the British
Library.

ISBN: 0–304–33274–7 (hardback)
       0–304–33276–3 (paperback)

Typeset by Action Typesetting Limited, Gloucester
Printed and bound in Great Britain by Biddles Limited, Guildford
and King's Lynn

CONTENTS

Preface   vi

1 Racist clouds   1
2 'It's not as bad as it's made out to be'   11
3 'Who does it? How can we stop it?   19
4 Telling tales   27
5 Case studies   41
6 Statistics   63
7 Mending hearts and broken promises   70

Appendix: Abuse survey   80
Index   85

PREFACE

This is a book about racism and the experience of the black sexually abused child. My intention in writing such a book is not to belittle the experience of white abused children, because abuse against any child is horrific. I feel, however, that it is time we acknowledged that for a child of colour, there are additional traumas, blocking the path towards healing.

Racist practice still exists in Britain. Lack of knowledge is apparent and awareness of racial groups and their cultures is low within childcare professions, placing any child from a minority ethnic group in a disadvantaged position. There are additional barriers which prevent a child from a non-white background disclosing abuse, particularly if the abuse is sexual. There appears to be a hidden agenda, which black and Asian people are encouraged to accept and collude with, that perpetuates the limits placed on them by racism. A black or Asian adult who is found guilty of abusing a child takes responsibility for the whole of their race.

During my years of experience as an anti-racist trainer and as a therapist working in the field of child sexual abuse, I became aware that I had few individual clients from cultures that were non-white or non-Jewish. While this could largely have been due to my being a white English woman, I still would have expected more people to come forward, given that there were few therapists for abuse in my area. I began to make enquiries of other therapists and the story was similar. So where were the surviving black adults and children going for support? The 1989 Children Act stipulates that all children should be given prime consideration with regard to their potential, irrespective of gender, cultural background, racial derivation, religion, academic ability, and physical and mental disadvantages.

It shall be the general duty of every local authority (in addition to other duties imposed on them by this Part)
a) to safeguard and promote the welfare of children within their area who are in need and

b) so far as is consistent with that duty to promote the upbringing of such children by their families, by providing a range and level of services appropriate to those children's needs.[1]

The definition of a child in need is: A child is disabled if he is blind, deaf or dumb or suffers from mental disorder of any kind or is substantially and permanently handicapped by illness, injury or congenital deformity or such other disability as may be prescribed; and in the Part – 'development' means physical, intellectual, emotional, social or behavioural development; and 'health' means physical or mental health.[2]

This should ensure that appropriate measures are being taken to support and sustain children and their families in cases of sexual abuse by making available to them professionals from a similar background or, where this is not possible, professionals with adequate cultural and ethnic awareness training who will be of positive use. How many children or adults from black and Asian backgrounds would be needing such support? Research into this issue has indicated that the number of minority children facing abuse is a similar percentage of their population to that in the white population.[3]

The purpose of this book is to see how deeply racism is affecting the provision of support and care for the abused black child, the prevention of disclosure of abuse by such children, and what we as a society can do to redress the balance. Do we still really think that certain practices are acceptable despite their obvious damage to the child involved, simply because they are seen as 'traditional'?

The widely held perception that it is normal for little black girls to be sexually manhandled by their fathers, grandfathers, uncles and friends of the family is one of the most damaging myths with which survivors have to contend. Not least because there appears to be little inclination or interest in changing this unhealthy state of affairs.[4]

Are we still at that stage in our own racism where we truly believe that members of different cultures with different skin tones have a genetic mental instability which disallows their awareness of the damage being done to their children from outside and within? Do we still accept without question that the problem lies in the culture of a person and not in the prejudice that perpetuates that belief?

The terms 'culture', 'ethnic groups' and 'race' are frequently used to express very different ideas about society.... Reber (1985) defines 'culture' as 'the system of information that codes the manner in which the people in an organised group, society or nation interact with their social and physical environment'. Reber also emphasises that 'culture' pertains only to non-genetic characteristics and that people must learn these systems and structures. Different groups of people such as anthropologists, psychiatrists or politicians, are able to use the term 'culture' for their own diverse purposes. Sashidharan (1986), for example, has observed that in psychiatry, words like 'culture' and 'ethnicity' are not neutral terms; instead these words take on a politically loaded meaning. Fernando (1988) endorses this view when he asserts that 'culture' is used in psychiatry in an ethnocentric way. Consequently, non-Western cultures that are alien to psychiatry are themselves seen as pathological. In this way 'culture' becomes the 'problem' that accounts for the abnormal behaviour of the client.[5]

What do I hope to achieve?

I am often told by participants in my anti-discrimination practice workshops that they cannot see how they, as individuals, can change the situation. My response has always been to state that one pebble thrown into a still lake can cause a disproportionate amount of movement. Perhaps this is my time to be a pebble. I write this book with the earnest hope that all children, of whatever colour, culture or gender, will be supported and acknowledged in a way that is appropriate to meet their needs. For as long as power remains high on the agenda of human communication, there will be sexual abuse and rape.

Notes

1 Children Act 1989, Section 17(1). London: HMSO, 1991.
2 *Ibid.*, Section 17(11).
3 Refers to research carried out in America and Britain which will be discussed in subsequent chapters.
4 Melba Wilson, *Crossing the Boundary*. London: Virago, 1993.
5 Patricia d'Ardenne and Aruna Mahtani, *Transcultural Counselling in Action*. London: Sage, 1989.

CHAPTER 1
Racist clouds

This is a two-part chapter. The first part is devoted to definitions of the terminology I will use. I will also suggest how racism may have a bearing on the way children of colour who have been abused may view themselves and/or the abuse they have been, or are, subjected to. The second part will deal with evidence on how racism is used by various statutory bodies and professionals to free themselves from owning responsibility for an abused child or person, especially those deemed to be black.

Imagine a situation where, for whatever reason, you are considered to be an outsider by people from your community. How would you feel? How would you respond to those who assume your non-belonging? This is how one very self-assured 10-year-old Egyptian Muslim girl saw to it that her antagonists were faced with their own prejudices:

> "Can you speak English?"
> What an odd question I thought to myself
> Why's he asking me that?
> I've spoken a full sentence,
> I've repeated it twice.
> Let me repeat again but slower:
> 'Yes ... I ... can ... speak ... the ... lingo
> And ... no ... I ... don't ... play ... bingo.'
> Surely he understood that.
>
> "Can you speak English?"
> She asked with doubt
> Speaking with her lips in full pout.
> 'Yes I can'
> I said with glee
> For I knew what she was about to say.
> "Can you speak English?"
> She said once again.

For heaven's sake I won't repeat it again.

"Can you speak English?"
She asked me one night.
(Not again!)
So I said 'No, I can't'
She asked me when I'd come over to England.
'But I can't speak English' I said.
"Oh how silly of me." She said with a sigh.
"But you're speaking to me quite fluently."
'Exactly.' I said
As she turned bright red.

Could we always guarantee to respond with such positive attitudes? As a large community, we assume that, where we deem a person to be 'different', we are within our rights to behave in an overly familiar way towards them. Hence we are surprised and a little put out when a person with a physical disability refuses our offer of help, or a blind person isn't absolutely weeping with gratitude because we've pulled them across the road. Why do men, for example, feel it is incumbent on them to tell a female walking past to 'cheer up love, it may never happen'? Well, it did, as soon as they opened their mouths. Why do we presume it will be fine to feel a black child's hair without asking permission, just to check the difference between theirs and ours? Why do we have the arrogance to monitor what an overweight person is eating as if he or she shouldn't be consuming anything sweet? Why do we do it? The answer lies in the assumption that some people (namely the 'us') are afforded more privileges than others. This leads me back to the first topic of this chapter, definitions.

This section will convey to the reader the definitions of terms as I understand them and as I make use of them throughout the book.

Black

Any person with features and skin colour indicating a family derivation from Africa, the Caribbean Islands or South Asia. Even if they have mixed-race parentage, it is the skin colour that is the deciding factor. Politically speaking, most people who are not white European are considered black in a derogatory sense.

Culture

The identity which we have, based on memories, ethnicity, parenting and child-rearing attitudes, class structures, economy, gender roles, religion, etc. Cultures are neither superior nor inferior to each other. They evolve as the people in them evolve.

Ethnicity or Ethnic Identity

Characteristic of a group of individual people who share similar experiences in the form of customs, religion, language, nationality and, possibly, lifestyle. It would therefore be acceptable to identify a Caribbean ethnicity, or an Asian ethnicity, or an Irish ethnicity, and so on.

Minority Group

A group joined by religion, ethnicity or culture, which is numerically smaller than the predominant white population, in countries such as Britain.

Nationalism

A belief (with no factual basis) that allows one group or nation to assume superiority over others by virtue of language, lifestyle, accent, economic status, history of oppression, intellect, humour, etc. Thus English nationals might assume superiority over Irish nationals, or German nationals might assume superiority over Polish nationals.

Racism

The belief by white people that they are infinitely superior to black people in all aspects of culture, religion, intellect, beliefs, lifestyle, parenting skills, language, and so on. This belief was upheld in historical 'factual' accounts by white male scientists or philosophers who supported their arguments by referring to Christian teachings and included among their number Charles Darwin (*Origin of the Species* (1859)) and David Hume (a philosopher of some renown (1711–1776)).

Figure 1.1 is an example of their 'evidence' which abounded in the 1700s and 1800s and sadly, for a percentage of the population, is still regarded as fact. It could easily be an example of how 'facts' about the black peoples of the world are 'proved'.

In such a historical climate of prejudice, it is small wonder that racism is still holding court.

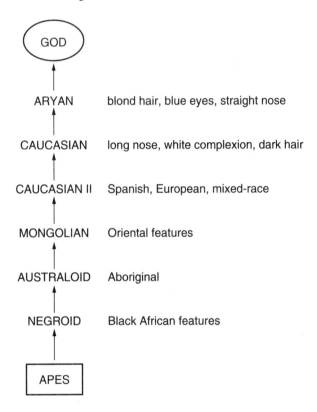

Figure 1.1

A black child who recognizes that what is happening to him or her is called abuse is faced with a dilemma. Such children have the trauma of the actual abuse, which will have affected their self-image as a child, how they view their gender, and their self-worth, compounded with whatever effect racism has on them as individuals. They may, for example, be disinclined to ask for help, particularly if the abuser was also black, in an attempt to prevent the white professionals and population from assuming that all black adults abuse black children and it is their own fault. In Melba Wilson's book *Crossing the Boundary*[1] she quotes examples of high-ranking

American scholars who insisted that racism was not damaging black communities and perpetuating child abuse, but that it was black women who caused it by not allowing their men to be dominant over them and their children. A similar argument was put about in Britain after the Second World War when men returned from fighting to find that women had achieved independence and status for themselves by doing 'war work'. They were blamed for men's low morale, not the fact that the economy was shot to hell, or that unemployment was high. It was a female problem inflicted on men.

If black children have been abused by a white person, they may assume, again, that this is all they are worth – and who would believe them anyway? Haven't they been given plenty of information about their low status?

> Children from ethnic minorities also can assume that their sexual abuse will not be taken seriously. If they are treated as if they don't matter, then why should their abuse matter? As Edgar Hoover, former and long-term head of the FBI said, 'Some niggah bitch gets herself raped.' If they could be sold and murdered, why not raped.[2]

Even if such children were to seek help, what could they expect? Have the supporting services thought deeply enough about how to offer support to a black child? Are there adequate numbers of staff trained to meet any child's needs from whatever cultural and ethnic background? Is there recognition of the cultures of all children in local authority care and are there the means to deal with them accordingly?

Tasnim Yawar, social work course director at Kingston University, carried out a survey of ninety-one social services departments throughout Britain to discover how many Muslim children, and of what age, were in local authority care. He wanted to find out whether the staff had specific awareness training in the needs of Muslim children, such as religion, diet and cultural history. He also made enquiries as to whether any of the authorities had established contact with local Muslim organizations or potential Muslim foster parents. He discovered that only three of the departments had a Muslim member of staff and a fourth had nurtured a good working relationship with a local Muslim children's home.

> Introducing the findings, director of the Islamic Foundation, M. Manazire Ahsan, said there is a widely-held assumption that Muslim young people, particularly those of South Asian origin,

are seldom taken into care because of their traditional extended family which enables substitute care to be provided if parents cannot look after their children. 'Such as assumption, although true in some cases, fails to take into consideration the fact that most Muslims in Britain do not have an extended family network.'

The report showed that there are 127 Muslim children and young people up to the age of 16 who are in care. This gives an average of 1.4 children for each of the 91 Social Services Departments which took part in the survey. Assuming the Muslim population in the U.K. is one and a half million, the number of Muslim children in care is 1.2 per 10,000 of the Muslim population. Yawar found local authorities' ethnic monitoring records were poor. A large number were unable to identify Muslim children from their records of young people in care. 'Most do not make any distinction between Muslim and non-Muslim children.' Yawar said. 'They are labelled depending on the colour of their skin. Muslims come from Nigeria and Trinidad and because they happen to be black, they are categorised as black.'[3]

There was also a discrepancy in the attitude staff had towards female Muslim children, seeing them as oppressed compared to Western girls. This is a damaging stereotype which denies the girls the ability to be anything but passive chattels under the domination of the male members of their society. If children feel that a large percentage of who they are is ignored, it would not be difficult to work out that invisibility is the next step. The Children Act[4] emphasizes that in order for a change in circumstances to take place, whether by those private individuals who apply for parental responsibility, or for the child to be accommodated by the local authority: 'The age, gender, background and characteristics of the child which the court considers relevant (including race, religion and culture)' should be taken into consideration. What happens in reality is that black and Asian children are rarely afforded this recognition, due in some part to financial constraints which affect staffing and accommodation available, but also because some authorities don't fully acknowledge the importance of a child's identity.

If a white child is removed from his or her family because of sexual abuse, that child can attempt to start life again somewhere else. The culture of that 'somewhere else' will be very similar to what they left behind, but that wouldn't be noticed. The culture itself wouldn't 'trigger' past unpleasant memories of abuse.

But if a child is part of a despised community, that community is like an oasis in the desert. Its sights, sounds and aromas make it unique and therefore identifiable to the child and everyone else. If that culture is associated through memory or through internalised oppression with abuse, and cannot be separated out, then every time the child touches that safe place, pain will be felt. There will be no safe place.[5]

When, through no fault of their own, children are alienated from their cultural environment, they experience severe psychological damage which may never be repaired. Racism seeps into black children's lives so insidiously that, for many, they don't even realize it is there, and they take upon themselves the responsibility for being so different.

Child sexual abuse is the misuse of power by an individual (usually male) against a child. Whether the child is black or white it does harm. If the child is black, however, it does particular harm because of the added dimension of race. When a white child is sexually abused they think they are bad and dirty. When a black child, especially a girl child, is abused, she thinks she is bad, dirty and an affront to the race, both in sexual terms and in terms of being black and female. She thinks, too of the message it will send to white society if she tells.[6]

There is the additional problem of the type of racism which allows the white professionals to take a step back from responsibility. Audrey Droisen[7] cites such an example. A white health visitor told her and other white colleagues about a child from a Nigerian family who had developed gonorrhoea as a result of sexual assault in Nigeria; the health visitor had accepted the family's word and did not take any further action in case she offended the family, despite her responsibility towards the child. Her colleagues did not challenge this but took it as read that intrusion into black family life is taboo. Whichever way we look at this, it is a form of racism and is harmful. How many other children have been neglected by those cast in a caring role?

According to the Children Act, when someone believes that a child may be being abused, they should report their concerns. There are powers afforded to the police and social services to investigate the suspicion so that the welfare of the child remains paramount. In my opinion, it should be an offence punishable by law when a professional in the caring sector ignores the signs or symptoms of abuse in children of any colour.

> Addressing child sexual assault, as with child abuse, means for us to address racism. When Africans were first enslaved it was necessary for Europeans to evolve a philosophy of justification. In the process well over 75 million Africans were left at the bottom of the sea. These basic assumptions inform this society's interaction with us to this very day. Ideas which have become enshrined in this country's culture.... The abused child feels responsible for what has taken place. The abused child feels dirty, the abused child feels alone, the abused child feels angry. The abused child feels negative about themself and all these feelings feed into the impact. An African child who has been sexually abused can confuse this whole experience with what it is to be an African, the outcome is very often a compounded self hate.[8]

An aspect of racism which needs to be addressed is the 'colour-blind' approach. There are those among us who claim to 'treat all children alike' or say that a child who is abused will suffer the same traumas, so therefore the colour of the skin is immaterial. If this line is taken, it then allows all children to be supported in exactly the same way, by the same people, in the same establishments and for the same length of time. You wouldn't be able to tell the difference, would you? There is no difference in colour, so a black child supported by white workers, whether in a residential environment or at home, will not see this behaviour as a reflection of how society views black people. If the child does, then he or she is just being silly. We all live the same lives, worship the same deity, eat the same food, oil our bodies in the same way, brush our hair the same way, have the same health problems, such as sickle-cell anaemia, and are all treated fairly when in trouble. Remember how ridiculous it was when Mick Johnson[9] from *Brookside* became upset when the police were investigating his immigrant status. After all, it happens to everyone.

Andrea Dworkin, in her book *Pornography*, makes the point that skin colour, i.e. black skin, often becomes a sex object in itself.

> Sometimes objectification is clearly sinister, for instance when it signifies, as it often does, racial hatred. As Robert Stoller points out, not necessarily with aversion, '... some people need the

excremental ... to choose people they consider fecal (e.g. black, Jewish, poor, uneducated, prostituted).' ... The relationship between the supposedly silly and commonplace objectification of blondes as beautiful and the sinister objectification those considered in some way filth is, of course, a direct one: the same value system is embodied in this range of sexual obsession, sexual response.... There is the specific sexual value of the black woman in pornography in the United States, a race-bound society fanatically committed to the sexual devaluing of black skin perceived as a sex organ and a sexual nature. No woman of any other race bears this specific burden in this country.[10]

If we have any hope of putting our house in order, we have to accept that racism exists and that it festers in every aspect of life. It is present in institutions such as mental health care, the prison service, education. When parents in a northern town fought against their children being exposed to an Asian language, which the majority of children attending the school spoke as their first language, I wonder what they were protecting their children from? Why did they feel it was detrimental to their children's learning? Couldn't they see that exposure to any challenge to learning is an enhancing experience? Would they have done the same if the language had been French? Look at how we describe some of the languages from the Caribbean – for example, pidgin English, fractured English, broken English – when in reality they are special languages in their own right. The problem with such an emotive subject as racism is that we all have our own views about what is considered to be offensive and who will be offended.

I would like at this point to remind you about the definitions at the beginning of this chapter (pp. 2–3). If you are black, you have probably been subjected to racism. If you are white, you have probably been racist in your time, by thought, word or action. The grandparents who, when their mixed-race, beautiful grandchild asked them why she wasn't the same colour as them and her Mum, told her she would 'grow out of it' were being appallingly racist; not only had they confirmed that to be black was undesirable and inferior, but that it was like a disability which one could lose through maturity. How much worse it must be for the black, sexually abused child to be alone, voiceless and flawed in an all-white world.

Notes

1 Melba Wilson, *Crossing the Boundary*. London: Virago, 1993.
2 Audrey Droisen and Emily Driver, *Child Sexual Abuse, Feminist Perspectives*. London: Macmillan, 1989, p. 5.
3 'Caring about faith. A survey of Muslim children and young persons in care'. Review by Catriona Marchant of a paper by Tasnim Yawar. *Community Care*, 2 September 1993.
4 Children Act 1989, Section 1(2). London: HMSO, 1991.
5 Droisen and Driver, *Child Sexual Abuse*, p. 6.
6 Wilson, *Crossing the Boundary*, p. 7.
7 Droisen and Driver, *Child Sexual Abuse*.
8 Wilson, *Crossing the Boundary*, p. 8.
9 Mick Johnson is a fictitious character in the Channel 4 television soap, *Brookside*. He is black and was born in Liverpool, but when he created a fuss by speaking out, his residential status was checked and his passport taken away.
10 Andrea Dworkin, *Pornography: Men Possessing Women*. London: The Woman's Press, 1981 (reprinted 1988), p. 9.

CHAPTER 2
'It's not as bad as it's made out to be'

I am a collector of myths, legends and fairy stories told in order to justify and rationalize non-action or an attack of sudden selective blindness where child protection issues raise their ugly heads. The ones I set before you here may sound familiar. There may even be some you yourself have used. They can be found in various forms in several child abuse manuals or in some training programmes. What I ask you to bear in mind is that myths, legends and fairy stories belong in the imagination and bear no relation to real life. Let's start off with a list of reasons why suspicion of child abuse might not be reported. These are not the only excuses and you may wish to add more.

It is cultural/subcultural. This is how 'these' families behave.
- This is racism and nationalism in its worst form. It allows groups of people to be separated into 'good' and 'bad', when in fact there is no culture which actively promotes child sexual abuse.

The children are used to it so it can't be doing any harm.
- For children who are aware that they are being abused and that no one is prepared to support them or help them make the abuse stop, the conclusion they come to is that they are worthless, fit only for sex; or worse, fit only for death. I have counselled many young people who turn to self-abuse either in the misguided belief that this is their worth, or to create a pain which is external and therefore real.

It's happening all the time.
- So what? That doesn't make child abuse acceptable.

The mother was sexually abused as a child so there's no chance that she would allow this to happen to her own children.
- If the mother has not been able to identify for herself all the signals of a potential abuser, or if she focuses on one person's behaviour (namely her own abuser) as the only source of danger, then her children may be at risk, as are children of non-abused parents.

I've known this family for years. If something like that was happening I would certainly have been aware of it.

- Most families where incest is regarded as a 'normal' event in life do not necessarily give out obvious signals, and the abuser has probably convinced others that the problems lie with the victim. I remember talking to the mother of two abused daughters at a conference on child abuse issues and she told me that throughout her daughters' teens, her husband had persuaded her that the girls were unmanageable and they should not be trusted. He was a school medical officer; how could he not be telling the truth?

Boys are never sexually abused.

- Although, statistically, there may be more girls than boys reporting abuse, it does not mean that the number of male children being abused is nil.

Children mix up fact and fantasy, so it's probably not true.

- A child may have heard of the term 'abuse', but until it happens to him or her would be unable to tell in explicit detail what it means. A friend's daughter, aged 6, told her mother that she was 'sexing with her friend'. When her mother asked what that meant, the girl replied that it meant kissing under the blankets.

The victim told the story in a hesitant way so she must be lying.

- Most victims of long-term abuse find that theirs is a hazy story. So much happens over such a long period of time that details blur. It is often the realization that this was abuse which causes such behaviour.

The story was consistent / inconsistent, so it's a fake.

- As previous reply.

This is an attempt to get revenge over the mother / father / cohabitee.

- Check the detail.

She's lying to conceal the fact that she's having sex with her boyfriend.

- Young girls, particularly those whose abusers fear they may disclose or who have been made pregnant as a result of the abuse, are often subjected to this accusation. The rumour is always started by the abuser.

This child must be lying; the mother is horrified.

- We assume that mothers know what is happening to their children at all times, whether or not they are with the child. They are bound to be horrified, especially when the abuser turns out to be a trusted family friend. In these cases the build-up to abuse can be quite slow and deliberate; part of the plan is to win the complete trust of the parent.

Allegations of abuse are often false, but retractions are always true.
- When I worked for a national telephone help line for children I remember a young person who called to say he had been abused by his uncle. He had some mild learning difficulties but he knew that he wanted the abuse to stop. He was supported in this and he spoke to a social worker who helped him to tell his mother. Within a week, the boy had retracted his story, despite the amount of detail he was able to supply to back his account, and he phoned to say he was sorry and that he wouldn't lie again. He hadn't lied, but his mother and family had clearly put pressure on him to retract his statement.

The police will never take this seriously.
- Under the Children Act, the police are required to make enquiries into any reported suspicion of child abuse.

This family has suffered enough; let's forget the abuse.
- So we'll allow the abuse to continue, shall we?

The abuser has gone now, so everything's OK.
- How can we be sure there was only one abuser, and even if there was, what do we do about the damage he or she inflicted?

There was no actual penetration, so where's the harm?
- Sexual abuse is not always about penetration. The emotional scars from any form of abuse, whatever its severity, have long-term healing problems.

This was a one-off.
- The victim isn't able to be lucky enough to forget that easily.

It's best to keep quiet, as talking about such things creates more pain.
- Most victims say they felt that someone else understood the pain they had suffered if they were given permission to talk.

If we say or do anything, the family will fall apart.
- If we stay quiet, the children will fall apart.

Abusers just need to be forgiven; it is just a deviant sexual urge.
- It is the word 'just' that sums up how we still protect abusers and not their victims.

I may be wrong.
- If you are, the most you have done is to embarrass yourself a little.

Well, we blame the mother. After all, a man has needs.
- This is the excuse a judge allowed a man to use when he was accused of raping his daughter during his wife's pregnancy, and Ann Borrowdale[1] cites the case of a man who raped a deaf and dumb woman and was acquitted, as he was under the influence of drink.

Women, especially mothers, don't abuse children.
- Oh no?

Children don't abuse children.
- They do, and it invariably means that they themselves have been or are being abused by an older person.

The child is handicapped and doesn't have feelings.
- This myth has perpetuated abuse in residential homes for handicapped children for too long. It must not be allowed to continue.

The child could speak: why didn't she just say no?
- How can a child say no when adults, particularly parents, are constantly negating the word no from the child's vocabulary? Children don't say no to adults, they keep quiet, especially when parents like Fred and Rosemary West tell their children that 'all parents do this kindness to their children'.[2]

There must have been something the victim did to cause this behaviour in the abuser, it is so out of character.
- Very few rapists or child abusers act out of character; they are merely adept at hiding their true nature.

The difficulty with myths is that we sometimes believe them to be true. They become so ingrained as a way of life that no one, especially those suffering the consequences of such a belief system, questions their validity. There are, for example, stories which enable abusers within black communities to perpetuate their crimes. These stories may be held as fact. It is assumed that incest is accepted in black cultures, and that a man shows love to his daughter by being the first to initiate her. This is the double-bind of racism, because many people from those black communities may also believe these fairy stories. Their history belongs to the days of slavery and indenting. The slave-owners or landlords often considered that young black virgin girls were theirs by right, and the fathers of such girls would attempt to alleviate the pain for their daughters in the only way they knew. This was also considered the norm in Britain, dating back to medieval times and through to the early part of this century. Where there was a lord of the manor and serfs or domestic servants, it was anticipated that the man would take what he considered to be his.

There are other myths about the ability of black victims, especially females ones, to cope with anything dealt to them. The ability of black women to show strength in the face of adversity is probably a direct result of having to face such traumas alone. The way words can influence how we view the different sexes and colours of skin is often prejudicial. We call black-skinned women 'exotic', we call female children 'flirts' and encourage them to look away, then look at us again in a coquettish manner, a clear invitation or permission-giving, to some, to commit rape or abuse. We call children 'precocious', which means they are behaving in a manner in advance of their age, again a good-enough reason to abuse. We accuse female children of desiring a sexual relationship with their father and believe this to be so. We blame victims of rape for the way they are dressed, for going out by themselves. We also blame female victims for not controlling the man.

> The male conceit that women have sexual power (cause erections) conveniently protects men from responsibility for the conse-quences of their acts, especially their acts of sexual conquest.[3]

Try this quiz for yourself to see what makes you feel uncomfortable and what makes you feel OK. Read each statement and then decide whether it sounds safe or unsafe. As you read through the statements and make a decision, think about how you justify the decision you have made.

1. Father shows his daughter his penis to 'educate' her.

   safe/unsafe
2. Children watch their parents have sex.

   safe/unsafe
3. Mother lets her husband have sex even though she doesn't feel like it.

   safe/unsafe
4. Mother shows off her young son's penis to her family and friends.

   safe/unsafe
5. Male members of the family, including the father, make fun of a girl's developing body.

   safe/unsafe
6. Father shows his son how to use a condom.

   safe/unsafe
7. Mother encourages her daughter to wear make-up and to dress in an adult fashion.

   safe/unsafe
8. Mother shows her daughter how to use a tampon.

   safe/unsafe

9. Father inserts his finger into his 3-year-old daughter's vagina when bathing her.

safe/unsafe

10. Parents forbid their 16-year-old daughter to go out with boys.

safe/unsafe

11. Mother pulls back her uncircumcised young son's foreskin when bathing him.

safe/unsafe

12. Father/mother bathe with their 4-year-old child.

safe/unsafe

13. Father kisses his 13-year-old daughter on the mouth at bedtime.

safe/unsafe

14. Mother kisses her 13-year-old son on the mouth at bedtime.

safe/unsafe

15. Father has an erection when cuddling his 2-year-old daughter.

safe/unsafe

16. Father initiates his daughter in sex as it 'will be less painful' for her.

safe/unsafe

17. An 11-year-old girl has a period and doesn't know what it is.

safe/unsafe

18. A young boy is circumcised according to cultural tradition.

safe/unsafe

19. A young girl is circumcised according to cultural tradition.

safe/unsafe

20. Parents make jokes about their 8-year-old son dressing in female clothes.

safe/unsafe

Your responses probably have some relevance to the religion and culture which you identify as yours; for example, some cultures and religions practise male and female circumcision. The question is, is it safe? The answer depends on your belief system, your willingness to challenge and question, and whether this has also happened to you. Female circumcision has been illegal in this country since 1985. It may still happen here; if it does and the perpetrators are discovered, they can be prosecuted. It is a cultural tradition which needed to be challenged. There is now a body of people from both the Muslim and Jewish religions who are beginning to doubt the efficacy of male circumcision. The first challenge is usually made after a child suffers enough harm to be killed, and this has happened with circumcision of both genders. There is also discrepancy as to the history of the act. For some, it has a religious validity; for others, it separates the cultures and therefore should be maintained. For people like myself who do not have those traditions to consider, it appears barbaric and abusive. I defy anyone who has witnessed either of these two acts to still maintain that it is pain-free and harmless.

There are some traditions which are no longer necessary to spiritual life, a good example of which is Chinese footbinding, which was carried out on young girls for over a thousand years. The toes were forced under the soles of their feet and bound so tightly that they experienced pain at every movement. This had no real religious or healthy cultural significance; it was merely a form of sexual slavery which men perpetuated and enjoyed.[4] There is doubt now whether circumcised males help to prevent cervical cancer in their female partners, and there are also questions about the hygiene benefits of having a circumcised penis. We should not be frightened to challenge; it allows the cultures to evolve and maintain an individuality based on real beliefs and ideals.

There are myths which abusers use to fool both themselves and those who may accuse them of abuse. This final section invites you to assess for yourself how easily this can be achieved.

Abuser statement: We had special times which we spent together.
Victim statement: I used to cry when I heard his/her footsteps on the stairs.
Abuser statement: I knew that look; she/he couldn't hide their feelings.
Victim statement: Every time they looked at me I tried to avoid eye contact, so they wouldn't think I was willing.
Abuser statement: Black kids enjoy that sort of thing, they know what they like.
Victim statement: I felt that it was my fault because of my colour. I wished I was white so it wouldn't happen.
Abuser statement: I was the only one to pay any attention to them. I feel you have to offer love to these problem kids.
Victim statement: I tried really hard to make myself ugly so they would leave me alone.
Abuser statement: My wife was never interested in sex after a few years.
Victim statement: I wished my Mum would have helped me.
Abuser statement: He's my little man.
Victim statement: I used to feel sick when she got into bed with me.
Abuser statement: We had special games we used to play.

Victim statement: He used to make me put it in my mouth.
Abuser statement: Why did he always get an erection then?
Victim statement: I hated my body for letting me down like that.

If we continue to allow myths to dictate how we live our lives without question, we are just as guilty as those who are more vociferous in their prejudiced beliefs. The old saying about evil being perpetuated by good men (and women) doing nothing is very true. It is not enough just to sigh and disclaim all responsibility for the world in which we live. It is necessary to become self-challenging, to become 'pro-active' (to use a politically correct term). Those of us who work in the area of child protection owe it to the children to become more aware of the individual needs of children which includes cultural and religious enlightenment. Chapter 3 suggests how this can be achieved.

Notes

1   Anne Borrowdale, *Distorted Images*. London: SPCK, 1991. There are many newspaper reports about the excuses allowed for this aspect of sexual violence. In March and July 1994, the *Guardian* reported two separate instances, the first of a man cleared of raping and assaulting his wife. The judge told the jury: 'You ought not to confuse lack of consent with a wife not wanting it, not enjoying it or not feeling like it, but letting it happen. Many a wife submits not through fear of violence, but because that's what she is used to doing and that's what she thinks she ought to do.'
    The second instance reported the judge who, at a rape trial in 1993, described the 9-year-old victim as 'not exactly an angel'. In that case, he gave the rapist two years' probation.
2   The step-daughter of Rosemary West and daughter of Fred West, interviewed by Independent Television on 16 November 1995.
3   Andrea Dworkin, *Pornography: Men Possessing Women*. London: The Women's Press, 1988.
4   There is an excellent description and some historical perspective on foot-binding in Andrea Dworkin's book, *Woman Hating* (New York: Dutton, 1974).

CHAPTER 3
'Who does it? How can we stop it?'

There are two important questions here. The brief answer to the first is that anyone can abuse a child, and if they are so inclined, at this stage in child protection awareness, there is little that can be done to prevent such an occurrence. Child abuse recognizes no cultural taboos, no religious boundaries, no financial restriction or wealth, no health issues, no colour ban. It is sometimes even easier to abuse children within a restricted religious or cultural code. There have been several accounts recently of Catholic priests found guilty of sexually abusing children, male and female, who kept their victims silent with the unspoken commandment of 'Honour thy priest, whatever he does to you, no one will believe the word of a child'.[1] The Catholic Church has colluded with this for many years. Any person who has the mantle of responsibility for children's spiritual, educational, health or environmental welfare is afforded a power that can be distorted if they are perpetrators of abuse. Abusers have been targeting victims for years; we make it easy for this to continue. The Christian religion bases its value system on the acceptance that we are all born with sin. We are then expected to live the rest of our lives atoning for this in some way so that, by the time we die, we are hopefully fit to take our place in heaven. When a baby is born, the perfection of the human form is so evident, and the willingness of each baby to trust implicitly each person it is brought into contact with and its genuine joy in being itself convinces me that this attitude is misguided and dangerous.

An article printed in the *Guardian* begins with the caption: 'No hearing for boy who lacked God to swear by.' It continues:

Charges against a man accused of sexually assaulting a boy were dropped because the boy did not believe in God and could not give sworn testimony to the Tasmanian supreme court, a newspaper said yesterday.

The Australian newspaper said Judge William Zeeman found the boy aged 12, had 'no expectation that God would punish him in this world or the next' and was therefore not fit to take an oath promising to tell the truth. Without the boy's testimony, the case against the man, aged 52, was weakened and the judge chose to drop the case.

In Darwin, meanwhile, police reported that about 40 aboriginal children have said they were sexually molested by a Roman Catholic teacher. Commander Terry O'Brien of the Northern Territory police crime division said the allegations came from members of the Tiwi group, who live on Bathurst and Melville islands north of Darwin.[2]

Here, the consequence of stating your lack of belief in God is double victimization.

Anne Borrowdale[3] mentions in her book a survey carried out into a variety of cultures. Those which were more 'rape-prone' tended to be the ones where there was belief in a male supreme being. She asks the question, is there a link between man's desire for dominance and an all-powerful male deity? As child abuse and rape are still very much a masculine trait, this theory would appear to hold water. It gives enlightenment to those critics of the matriarchal cultures of some black groups such as Caribbean families where life very much revolves around the female carers. These women are castigated for working away from the home, for being independent enough to have their own employment, for being strong enough to survive without a permanent male partner. As Melba Wilson[4] states, we need to remember who abuses children, who fails to protect the children by satisfying their own lust after power and the intention of causing pain, and not to look around for yet another scapegoat.

One of Britain's most senior Muslim priests was yesterday jailed for 11 years for a series of rapes on a schoolgirl and two other women. Ghulam Rasool Chishty was told by Judge Robert Lymbery: 'You were a high priest in the great Islamic faith and tradition. People turned to you for help thinking they were secure with you.' Detectives involved in the case believe Chishty may have raped many other women before his reign of debauchery was ended by the courage of a 15 year old Muslim girl who risked ruining family honour and being shunned by her community to tell her teacher what had happened to her. Her story gives a fascinating insight into the trauma of a girl caught between two cultures.[5]

The story goes on to say how the girl's parents had asked the priest for help when they felt their daughter was becoming too westernized. She had been born in Britain, so while she acknowledged her culture and religion, she wanted the freedom to be her own person. The priest persuaded her family that she was sick. Apparently a trick he used to demonstrate this was to place a piece of silver foil (smeared with a chemical that reacted to air by producing heat) on the back of a person's hand and tell them that if they were ill, they would feel a burning sensation. The girl knew that he should not be raping her every time she visited him, but her culture dictated that priests were to be revered and for a while she felt she couldn't tell anyone. When she eventually disclosed and the trial was over, her parents were devastated by the betrayal of the holy man. Their daughter had lost trust in them as they had initially refused to believe her. It is thus important that we all ensure we don't begin to blame closed cultures for abuse. It can happen anywhere.

Newspaper headlines scream the stories:

'Race To Trap Evil Child Sex "Social Workers"' [6]
- An article about men posing as social workers who con their way into private homes by claiming to be council welfare officers investigating child sexual abuse reports, in order to examine the children of the families.

'Abuse Still Rife in Institutional Care Claims NSPCC' [7]
- Publishes claims by the NSPCC that the abuse of children in institutions goes unreported.

The question of who abuses children is as complex as it appears simple. 'Who' could be anyone: male, female, adult, child. The list of characteristics describing a 'typical' child sexual abuser includes suggestions that they have an inadequate personality, they have an exaggerated need to control, they do not form adult relationships easily, they have a subjective memory, they are manipulative, they are highly seductive, they have strong sexual performance needs. The list is seemingly endless. A word of caution is necessary here. Most research into the profile of a sex offender is carried out on those who are caught, tried and imprisoned for their crimes. They are also the ones who invariably claim to have been abused during childhood. I think we should begin to tell it like it is. An offender is an offender. There can be no acceptable excuse allowed. There can be no sympathy given. Sexual abuse and rape are acts of violence performed on the body but wounding the psyche. No one who has been victimized ever completely forgets. No one who has been victimized feels completely clean again. No one who has been victimized feels completely safe again without putting a vast amount of time and energy into the healing process. It is not fair that there are millions of victims who are obliged to put parts of their lives on hold while they clear out the mess imposed upon them by another. The process can take years, it can take a lifetime. How much more complicated, then, if the victim is black? Andrea Dworkin, in her book *Pornography*,[8] mentions in stark detail how the colour of a black woman's skin becomes the sex object. In effect, for some women and children of colour, there is no escape. She also reports the high incidence of black males who are raped and abused in the prison system. Racism has ways of making people of colour pay.

How do we prevent it from happening? The first step is to identify clearly the behaviour of a sexual abuser of children. This list of behaviours applies in the main to the serial abuser.

- Most abusers target a type of child either by gender, by physical appearance or, for some incest abusers, because they are 'property'. For most victims, there has been a gradual build-up in intensity of behaviour, culminating eventually in some form of penetration.
- Abusers tend to keep their victims isolated.
- The child labelled as a 'problem' by his or her parents may be trying to tell you something.
- The child who has few friends or who is not allowed to do the normal things other children do may be at risk of abuse.
- A child who is scapegoated by the family may be the target of an abusing parent. Incestuous parents don't necessarily abuse all their children.
- The child who has a 'special' relationship with an adult, especially a family friend, may also be victimized. These friends of the family may, when you stop to think about it, know lots about you, but you actually know the barest minimum about them.
- Most abusers at some time bribe their victims with gifts or special attention, making them important in the child's life.
- Most abusers normalize the relationship with the child in such a way that other adults may not necessarily identify abusive behaviour but feel uncomfortable when in the presence of the child and the abuser; lingering full-mouth kisses are not normal behaviour in any culture to my knowledge. Kisses on the mouth maybe, but it is the intensity which is the give-away.

- At some time, the abuser may become so confident about not being challenged that they may publicly display more overtly bizarre behaviour.
- There may be secrets between the abuser and the abused.
- The abuser has already allowed the child to take full responsibility for the abuse: 'You're the image of your mother, I can't help myself,' or, 'You know this is what you want.'
- Fear becomes a part of the secret relationship, and abusers know exactly how to keep children quiet.
- Most child abusers abuse more than once.
- Some abusers use religion as a silencer.
- Some abusers use sex as a punishment, others use it as a reward, or an aspect of play, or it may be carried out in silence with no explanation at all.
- All abusers of children are well aware of children's behaviour: how to silence them, how to make them feel guilty. They are power magnates.

Black children are often doubly confused by the dilemma of coping with their experiences of racism and being abused by someone who may be from their own culture or who may be from a different cultural group. Before we look at the developments necessary in the professional childcare industry (see Chapter 7) let's work out what a black child will need in order to survive the ordeal with some hope of recovery.

There is a list of suggestions summarized by Catherine Roberts[9] as part of a paper reviewing practice in the treatment of child sexual abuse. I am going to use that as a base, including other suggestions and enlargements as I work through it. In the main this will also be relevant for white children.

1   *A good sex education*
- An abused child is often confused about what happened to her body and the feelings that accompanied the abuse. For children from some of the more protective cultures, it is also important that they clearly understand what happened to them was not a result of their wickedness, nor has it spoiled them for adulthood. In Madras, for example, the first centre for abused children has only recently been opened. There is still the problem that girls who have been abused cannot marry, so they are considered to be worthless to their families. The abuse is often hushed up and not acknowledged.[10] There

has to be negotiation between keeping girls innocent and not giving them any information at all.

2   *Children should be given support in building their self-esteem*
  • For the black child, this is even more important. To be proud of who you are should not be the privilege of the non-abused child. Being black did not cause the abuse – the abuser caused it.

3   *Children who are abused often need to relearn certain social skills which may have been disrupted as a result of the trauma*
  • Being able to talk to one's peers, being able to converse with adults, is a vital part of a child's re-entry into the world of the normal.

4   *Assertiveness training should be an automatic consideration*
  • It empowers the child and allows him or her to seek support in an appropriate manner. It may also provide enough self-awareness to prevent subsequent potential abusers from victimizing the child.

5   *Awareness of roles, and the boundaries, will help the abused child see how the abuser stepped out of line*
  • It offers the black, abused child release from the responsibility of protecting the reputation of their culture, particularly if the abuser was from the same culture, and places the blame where it belongs. So if a white man abuses his child, the situation is looked at in terms of his individual problem. But if a black man abuses a child, racist stereotyping will point the finger at black culture.[11]

I would like to share another type of checklist with you. On one of the training days I attended in 1993 to enhance my awareness of the Children Act, the presenter, Dr Christina Lyons, made reference to assessment criteria which all local authorities, families, magistrates, etc. should adhere to when considering how best to assist a child. In 1984, a group of eminent psychiatrists, doctors and childcare specialists were invited to compile a list of conditions necessary for children to develop and thrive. This suggests that survival alone is not enough in any child's life, if there is to be any possibility of achieving his or her full potential. This is a brief summary of their proposals:

1   Every child needs care and protection.
2   Every child needs affection and approval.
3   Every child needs stimulation and teaching.
4   Every child needs discipline and control which is age-appropriate and consistent.

5   Every child needs opportunity and encouragement, which will gradually allow him or her to acquire autonomy.
   • If one of these criteria is missing from a child's life, he/she will probably be damaged.
   • If two or more of these criteria are missing from a child's life, he/she will have considerable difficulty growing into a stable, mature adult.

The emotional apathy of abused or criminal children, and their failure to empathize with those they torment in turn, is frequently remarked by all who deal with them: 'He was not afraid of me,' said a police interrogator of one of James Bulger's killers; 'he is not afraid of anyone as far as I can see.' The deviant young and those engaged in antisocial acts will themselves frequently refer to this lack of feeling. They call it being 'bored', and claim that relief of boredom is the reason for their violent or sensation-seeking activities, whose short-term satisfaction then condemns them to an ever-escalating search for the next sensation, the next 'high'.[12]

Rosalind Miles's book reflects the absolute damage caused to children through inadequate parenting, inappropriate management and adults' refusal to accept responsibility for children under their care. The comments on the cover of her book highlight the necessity for adults to take this responsibility seriously:

The number of serious crimes committed by children under 16 in Britain has soared by 54 per cent in the last ten years.... But to blame these children, Rosalind Miles argues, is a way of evading blame ourselves. Children are born innocent, harmless and powerless. If they grow up confused and ignorant, destructive and self destructive, then the society that produces them must be so too. Every day the children who do not get what they deserve become the adults that no society wants. And they can, with justice, turn to us and demand, 'What did we do to deserve this?'[13]

If we add the proposals presented by Catherine Roberts to the criteria for thriving, we have a better picture of what every child deserves and what abused children in particular urgently need.

Notes

1 Roman Catholic priests hit the headlines in 1993 when Father Samuel Penney was jailed for an extended term after having been found guilty of sexually abusing children over a twenty-year period (*Guardian*, 24 May 1993).
2 *Guardian*, 17 November 1993.
3 Anne Borrowdale, *Distorted Images*. London: SPCK, 1991.
4 Melba Wilson, *Crossing the Boundary*. London: Virago, 1993.
5 *Mail on Saturday*, 19 January 1991.
6 *The Sun*, 1993.
7 *Community Care*, 1992.
8 Andrea Dworkin, *Pornography*. London: The Women's Press, 1981.
9 Catherine Roberts, *A Review of Good Practice in the Treatment of Child Sexual Abuse*. Produced for Wandsworth Borough by Tedious Research, September 1988.
10 *Woman's Hour*. Radio 4, 2 September 1993.
11 Audrey Droisen and Emily Driver, *Child Sexual Abuse*. London: Macmillan, 1989, p. 24.
12 Rosalind Miles, *The Children We Deserve*. London: HarperCollins, 1995, p. 25.
13 *Ibid.*, cover.

CHAPTER 4
Telling tales

As you read the following accounts of personal experiences of sexual abuse, don't feel that you have to identify racism in every sentence. In what I hope is an honest presentation of how racism affects the experience of black abused children, you, like them, may not be clear that racism is part of the picture. But while you browse through these pages, keep asking these questions: Did these children receive appropriate support and guidance? Why else might they not have told? Who was there for the family? How many times was a black professional appointed to make some of the distances between cultures closer?

> It has been our experience that counsellors working across cultures flounder when they fail to take into consideration a wide range of knowledge that is culturally significant to their clients. Counsellors have no direct control over their clients' cultural experience but they can anticipate and provide the space for their clients to express themselves in counselling. Culture permeates and affects all aspects of human experience and behaviour.[1]

The stories have three different forms of presentation. Some have been taken directly from a questionnaire I sent to those who volunteered to share their experiences with me (see Appendix, p. 80); some are in the form of detailed letters; and some are interviews with those who were courageous enough to meet me face to face and talk in more detail. I would like to thank all who agreed to do this. I know how much pain it brought back. No one that I spoke to was at all scathing or curious that a white person would want to do this type of research, and again, for your honesty and trust, I thank you.

CASE STUDY

Female survivor. Age at present: 34
My cultural background is Caribbean and Christian. The abuse was carried out by a male family member. He was about 18 when the abuse began and I was about 9. It continued for four years. It stopped because he was caught lying on top of me by my auntie. He told me that if I said anything to anyone, he would kill me. So, because you are frightened, you do keep it to yourself. You pretend everything is normal. At the time I didn't think about culture, but yes, it was common in our family. I think that my mother and aunties were abused. My cousin was abused as a young boy by the same family member. Even my brother wanted to have a go at me, but it didn't get that far with him. He stopped abusing me when he was caught. My grandfather called him into the parlour and hit him with an iron bar. That was his punishment. Nothing was said about the matter again. As for me, I was beaten by my mother with a belt. My father said, 'Leave her, she will only do it again.' I was beaten very badly. I feel they protected him more than me and cared about how he felt more than I did. Even now, we never talk about it even though I need to. I am messed up inside. I feel every man I have been with is a sexual abuser in their own way. They only want you for one thing. Sex. I can never say I have enjoyed sex. I have always felt dirty afterwards. I have never received any support. In my life all I ever wanted was to be loved by my family. You didn't expect someone in your family to be having penetrating sex with a 9-year-old. As a result of that I have no peace within me. When I am having sex with any partner I have had, I pretend to be someone else, I pretend to climax when I know I haven't. I portray this woman who is very good in bed even though I feel so dirty. It is all an act. I have never been able to express how I really feel and it has affected me in every relationship I have ever had.

CASE STUDY

Female survivor. Age at present: 27
I am from a Caribbean background. I was 6 when the abuse began and 15 when it stopped. The abuser was a male family member aged 15 when he began abusing me. I used to have to stay at his

home when my parents went to work. He never threatened me, I just knew it was meant to be a secret and somehow what he was doing was not right. It is common in my culture but it is a taboo subject which is kept very quiet and within the family. I rarely have contact with the abuser now. I never disclosed the information to anyone and kept it a secret for many years. I actually told someone when I was 23 and I had met a young girl who reminded me of myself. I then became very depressed and disclosed my abuse. I recently received a ten-week counselling session with a counsellor of my own cultural background. I have done a lot of reading about sexual abuse for my own benefit. I am no longer receiving support. I did feel that while it wasn't an issue of culture, the fact that I was female played a large part in why I was abused.

CASE STUDY

Female survivor. Age at present: 26
I am Caribbean Christian. I was abused by a male member of my family. I was possibly about 5 when the abuse first started and he was young as well, he was 8. It carried on for fifteen years and only stopped when I left home. I never told anyone because I knew my family wouldn't believe me. I was never verbally or physically threatened but I was always scared about what he would do if I told anyone. I felt I would be betraying my race if I told, especially if I told white people. I left home and moved into my own flat. I live five minutes away from my mum and the abuser still lives with her. I choose not to speak to him or see him, but sometimes at family gatherings I have to be in the same place as him. I felt that it was because I was bad that this happened to me. I don't think sexual abuse of black children is recognized as much as the abuse of white children. It is often swept under the carpet. I feel that as a black person trying to come to terms with my experiences of being sexually abused as a child has been very difficult. I have faced disbelief from my immediate family and have been unable to talk about it within my church for the same reason. I found it difficult to find a black person to talk to about my experiences. I felt that white people did not and do not share our history or many aspects of our culture. Apart from feeling shame about talking to strangers about the abuse, I also felt that I shouldn't be talking to

white people about it. It took me a long time to find a black therapist that I am happy with, but there is a shortage of black
therapists who deal with sexual abuse. It does go unrecognized
and unchallenged in our communities.

CASE STUDY

Female survivor. Age at present: 24

I am African Christian. I was abused when I was 4 years old by a
family friend from the same cultural group. He was about 19 years
old. I believe that in general people underestimate the abilities of
a child to remember; I remember almost everything. My mum
had gone out and this boy was asked to mind my brother and me. I
was woken up and put towards the end of the bed. I remember
having a small hole in my knickers. I'm not sure if this was torn
wider but that was where he put his thing. My brother woke up
(he was about 6 or 7) and obviously knew what he was doing was
wrong and told him to stop. The abuser told him to shut up or he
would put his thing in his mouth. He stopped and told me to go
and pee in a potty I had in the room. It burnt. My brother told my
mum when she came home and she hit the abuser with a shoe. I
can remember her screaming at him, telling him to leave.
Although she told family members and a few friends, nothing else
was done. Those services were not available then and I doubt if
they are now. My mum and I were watching an Oprah (Winfrey)
show about child abuse recently and I asked her if she remembered the event. At first she pretended not to, then said: 'But he
didn't do anything.' My boyfriend, who has been supportive, said
I would have been too small for penetration to have taken place. It
might be true, but as far as I was concerned, it did happen. Age
shouldn't be an issue, children remember a lot. I think other
important aspects are how we think the events have manifested
themselves in our everyday life, our family background and if we
blame any member of the family for what happened. I was so
young I didn't appreciate the gravity of the situation. It was not
supposed to be part of our culture; that is why the consequences
are ignored.

CASE STUDY

Female survivor. Age at present: 37
I am from a Caribbean background. The abuse happened when I was about 7. There were several members of my community involved in the abuse and it went on every day for ten years. All the abusers were male and their ages ranged from 20 to 60. It stopped when I left the country. I didn't tell because I thought no one would believe me. I thought it was normal for adults to do things like that. I didn't know it was abuse and believed that every child was just like me. It couldn't have been abnormal because so many of them were doing it to me. I did not associate this with my culture; I could not read or write, so had no way of understanding beyond what was happening to me. The abusers had ways of enticing me with food and a small amount of money. They knew I would accept the food, as this was my only way of surviving due to neglect. I left the country when I was 13. I believed for a long time that it was my fault, as there was no one else to blame. In 1986 I started working on some of the issues by myself and now my outlook is very different. I know that I could never inflict such pain and stress on my own children or in fact any human being. I do understand now how and why the abuse took place and the reasons why I was so exposed to it. In a visit to my country, one of the abusers asked me to have a baby boy for him as his wife was too old to conceive and his only son had died. I had felt sick for most of my life. Nothing made sense until I put two and two together. The saliva, in my mind, was associated with sperm. By the time I was 14 I thought I was a prostitute; I had no other answer. I believe this still happens in my culture.

CASE STUDY

Female survivor. Age at present: 29
I am African Christian. The abuse began when I was 6. My male abuser was 17. It carried on for a six-year period. It stopped when I eventually fought back. I didn't tell anyone because when I was 7, my dad found us together and gave us the belt. I had no idea what my culture's attitude towards sexual abuse was, but I was confused as to whether it was right or wrong. The longer it went on, I accepted it as OK. Until I realized it wasn't and was strong

enough to defend myself. By this time my parents had separated and my mother worked. I was left alone in the care of my older brother. I still have contact with the abuser. Our relationship used to be false, out of necessity, but now I have forgiven him, because he was also abused and when he abused me he was very young. I hated him until I was about 18 or 19. I couldn't bear to be near him and hated the pretence. I have never had counselling for my problems but I get support from a close circle of friends and some family members. I feel that abuse of children from non-white cultures is unimportant or non-existent according to popular belief. I can't say whether culturally, in England sexual abuse is customary, but I know it happens and I think that in England it is a male domination problem. Some beliefs and traditions are OK in Africa, but it is widely known that not all the old traditions are acceptable as part of Western society.

CASE STUDY

Dear Val,
I am very glad that I did contact you. My boyfriend saw your advert and told me what it said. When I first met my boyfriend who is seven years older than myself, I think he saw right through me. He knew I had a serious problem and because of him I am a better person. I was around 7 when my mother met her boyfriend. This man was always looking at me and commenting on what a pretty girl I was. He soon moved in with my mother. When she was at work, he used to let all the rest of my brothers and sisters go off to school and keep me at home. I was made to stand on one leg and was beaten with a leather strap and sexually abused. I was told not to tell anybody otherwise I was going to be punished. He used to tell me he loved me and I was given money and sweets as a treat. He even tried to make me perform oral sex. I cried a lot and it still hurts me even now. I wonder sometimes now because I am a grown woman, if there wasn't anything I did to cause those horrible things to happen to me. Could I have done something to stop it? Some nights he would try to creep in bed with me. My sister who was a very light sleeper would wake up and scream. I am sure my mother knew what he was doing and said nothing because it meant more money for her cigarettes and drink. She did catch him a few times creeping round the house. I'm even sure she knew

about my father abusing his two elder daughters of mixed culture, whom she adopted as babies. Anyhow, the abuse from her boyfriend went on until the school got in touch with the Welfare about my attendance. When the social workers came round I told them about the abuse. They sent me outside of the living room. I saw my mother's face as I went out. She was upset. I heard her shouting at the social workers that I was lying about what I was saying because I wanted my father and her to get back together. Her boyfriend gave her money for us and all that shit. That day I was taken to a judge's house and placed in the care of a London borough. I was placed in a community home where I was bullied for a long time by a white girl. A few years later I was placed in the same home as my brother. He was placed in care because my mother was going on holiday to Jamaica. I was sent back home after a while but I never allowed him to touch me again even though he tried. My mother used to ask him to take me to school but I never let him anywhere near me. I used to run away from home and never used to like school. I used to run away to my father's place where I was abused also. He said, if another man was fucking his child, why shouldn't he. I never went to his house unless I knew his girlfriend or my older brother was there. My father abused me, not constantly, but when ever it suited him. I was sent to another home in Essex and I used to run away from there too. On my thirteenth birthday I was raped by my sister's ex-boyfriend. I never told anyone, not even my sister. I was a fugitive at 14. I was on the run from children's homes and only went to my mother's when it suited me. My family is the worst. I'm glad my youngest brother was born a boy.

I met my present boyfriend when I was nearly 16. We started going out together in 1985 and moved in together by the end of the year. We now have two girls aged 7 years and 18 months. I have not spoken to my parents for three years and have no plans in the near future to do so. When I have seen my mother's boyfriend, I have driven by without acknowledging him. I told my brother about the abuse last year and he said I should have told him at the time. But what could I have said? I am at present studying towards a counselling qualification. I am still upset about being abused and I know I didn't have the right things said or done for me. I hold my parents, the boyfriend, and Social Services responsible for that. I know that I should have been offered counselling and educational support. The hurt does not go away. Day by day I am trying to put things in their place, and having my boyfriend around helps a great deal, as do my children whom I live for.

CASE STUDY

Robyn

Robyn was 5 and her first abuser was 9. She was not aware of the incident as being abusive as she was growing up. She just knew it wasn't right. At age 18 she was raped by a family friend when she was sleeping. She told her family, but they blamed her for causing the rape. The family don't talk about their business easily, even amongst themselves, and it is only now that she feels her innocence is being acknowledged. Robyn is now a social worker in an establishment working with troubled youngsters. She was sexually abused by a 14-year-old client. He was a known abuser and had demonstrated abusive and aggressive tendencies in his previous residential home. She feels she should have been warned so that she could have taken appropriate preventative steps and thus saved herself from such a trauma. Because of her experiences and the subsequent career she has chosen, Robyn is convinced that adolescents who were abused have more difficulty telling someone about their problems than younger children. The vicious circle of abuse has already been reinforced and there is no way of detecting which youngster has been abused and which one is more likely to abuse in turn. It is this continuous circle which concerns her most.

CASE STUDY

Heather

Heather came to Britain from the Caribbean with her parents. When she was 5, her mother went to America to work. She was sent to live with her aunt and uncle in the north of England. Her uncle, aged about 38, began to insert his finger into her vagina during bath time. As she grew older, he would do more things to her so that by the time she was 14 he was attempting penetration. Eventually her mother returned from America and Heather went home. She grew up believing that her uncle abused her because she was his favourite niece. It was only years later, when her niece was playing with her daughter, that she learned that her uncle had done this to all the little girls he came into contact with including his own children. Heather managed to 'forget' about the abuse until four years ago. She now realizes that she has survived through sheer determination. It became clear that the family must have been aware of the uncle's activities but they had all taken an unspoken vow to keep it secret. She couldn't be the only one to try to tell. Her retribution to herself was to be sexually promiscuous during her teenage years, collecting men like other children might collect stamps.

Heather now works in a residential home in the private sector for black children who have been victimized or who exhibit challenging behaviour. Her feelings are that there shouldn't be so many family taboos allowed to protect the family abusers, especially when little girls are being abused so much. There should be more information available about the signs and symptoms for black families in a variety of languages. There should be more resources made available for the children, their families and the professionals who work with them. This should include black-awareness training, self-help videos for black children, books and parent packs. She also feels there should be more statutory organizations skilled in supporting the black child and the family instead of having to rely on charitable bodies.

Heather appears to have managed to overcome the damage the abuse inflicted on her, by making full and appropriate use of her own experiences to support others. The important thing for her is that she can now leave the anger behind, in the past where it belongs.

CASE STUDY

Irene

Irene is African. She was abused by her father when she was small and she and her sister were placed in the care of the local authority due to his physical abuse of her. The sisters returned home when Irene was 7. The abuse continued and although she went to school with horrific bruises inflicted by both parents in a bid to silence her, no one at the school was prepared to support her or acknowledge the injuries which at times were so severe she could hardly lift her desk lid. She was labelled as a problem. The sexual abuse worsened, to the extent that Irene took herself to Social Services for help. She was examined by a Harley Street doctor and her father was arrested. According to the police and the doctor there was no evidence of sexual or physical abuse, and the case, which lasted for three years, was not proved. Irene is now in a bed and breakfast hostel round the corner from her family and refuses to have any contact with her parents. Her sister, who is now 15, has already had a nervous breakdown and Irene is very concerned about her. When she herself was 15, Irene was still trying to overcome the night-time fears she suffered from as a result of the threats used by her parents to keep most of the abuse quiet.

Irene feels bitter towards the school, which refused to see what was in front of their eyes, as well as towards her parents. She tried to heal herself by seeking out a black counsellor, but the cultural differences between them were too great and all she received from the counsellor were contradictions about how she felt and how she should feel about her family, the African traditions and her culture. When I visited Irene, she had recently resigned from a very good job because she is still unable to sustain any prolonged contact with people. This has become a pattern for her during her adult years. There is also a question about how long her boyfriend is prepared to tolerate her behaviour, which prevents her from going out often and prompts her to keep the curtains at her windows permanently closed. She remains suspicious of everyone she meets, and therefore cannot keep friendships alive.

CASE STUDY

Male survivor. Age at present: 34
I am from a Caribbean/Christian background. I was abused by a male family friend when I was 8 years old. He was 18. The abuse continued for about a month. I told my father but he said I must have been dreaming. The abuse stopped when we moved house. I have had no other contact with the abuser. Shortly after the abuse stopped, the abuser came to see me in my new home and my father made him to understand he was not welcome. I looked on this person as a brother. I am still upset that my father didn't believe me at the time, even though he does now. Since I remembered the experience I feel damaged in some way. I started to see a

counsellor on a weekly basis, but he moved house without warning and our sessions stopped. I told a girlfriend about the abuse and she was supportive at the time, but when we split up, she used the information to humiliate me. I find it difficult to trust people now. I believe that the abuse of non-white children is passed over as unimportant. There is no knowing how this affects future relationships. I wouldn't know how to act if I saw my abuser again.

CASE STUDY

Dear Val,
I am now 25. I was aged between 5 and 10 when my Grannie's lodger began to abuse me. He was about 50 at the time. We are both from the same Caribbean background. The abuse lasted for eight or nine years until I was 13. It stopped then, because my Grannie went back to Jamaica. I didn't tell, but I'm not sure why. He never threatened me but I do remember being scared to tell anyone about it. My abuser was a religious man and so was my Grannie. Maybe that had something to do with my not telling. I felt that I had done something wrong and it was my responsibility to fix it and correct the wrong doing, so I never said anything.

When my Grannie sold the house he had no choice but to find somewhere else to live. I considered that it happened to me because I was female. It is clear that your research is aimed at the cultural aspect of abuse and, speaking for myself, it is not an angle I have ever considered before reading this questionnaire. To be a child abuse victim is a highly traumatic and personal experience that has long-term effects that are very far reaching as I am sure you can appreciate. However, I felt that the questionnaire ignored me as I never told at the time the abuse took place. Neither did I get or seek help for it until many years later. My counsellor was a white female connected with the student social services department. She did help me a bit, in that it was the first time I could sit and talk about me with the focus being on me trying to understand my confused emotions at the time. The sessions lasted eight weeks, during which time I completed a 'victim recovery sheet'. The result at the time was quite positive but it still doesn't really help me to stay motivated when I get depressed and sometimes suicidal. Sometimes I see myself as a social chameleon, but when my feelings/emotions (sometimes I don't even know what to call it) get unbearable, I just retreat into myself and lock myself away in case I contaminate the people around me. I'm not even really sure why I am telling you these things, but it is making me try to make sense out of my confusion at this time. I hope you understand but if you don't, then it really doesn't matter because it's helping me to try and get to know who I really am. You wanna know something? My abuser stole something from me but what I can't work out is what it is. The counsellor said it was my innocence and my right to be a child but in all honesty, I think it is more than that. Sometimes I just feel so empty that it causes me to question what my purpose in life is. People I have asked have said that they have the same questions of life and have no readily available answers. So where does that leave me and my questions of self-doubt? What made me finally go for counselling was that I tried to end my life, although I will admit I didn't do it properly. Who is to say that if I didn't take more of my Mum's painkillers that I wouldn't be here today. It was on my mind at the time, to finish the job with paracetamol, but the phone rang. I look back to that time and wonder if there was someone looking down on me, who took care of me. I would like to get some more counselling or just have someone to talk to about what happened. I sometimes wonder if there is really something wrong with me, especially as I can't pinpoint exactly how I feel or even what it is I am feeling. Is it normal for a victim to feel this way?

I am in my last year of my degree and I have no clear idea what I really want to do. I'm 23 for God's sake. This cannot be normal, it scares me that I will blame the lack of control in my present life on what happened to me when I was younger. What is worse, I can't see the link between the two, so why is one influencing the other? It's said that abuse victims can push all bad memories into their subconscious minds while still always being aware of what happened. It's hard for me to remember most of the details of the abuse. At times I ask myself if it really did happen.

CASE STUDY

Female survivor. Age at present: 44
I am Pakistani. I was born in Pakistan and was the only female child in a large extended family. My culture and religion are Muslim. When I was about 9, an uncle began touching me, and

eventually having full penetrative intercourse with me. I couldn't tell anyone because he had already told me what would happen to me for letting him do this terrible thing that only husbands and wives do together. Somehow, more uncles seemed to know what I was being used for, and they all began to use me in the same way. This continued until my parents arranged a marriage for me. My parents would not have forced me to marry the man if I hadn't wanted to, but I was so relieved to escape that I wouldn't have refused. He was much older than me. We came to Britain and I discovered that he was also an abuser, but in a physical way. I have very little contact with my family now, because they are so far away. I now have children whom I love very much and they have made my life worth something. My husband's health is failing and while that is sad, it does mean he no longer has the energy to beat me. He relies on me more now. I have a career, I have my self-respect and I have my children. My sadness is that within my culture, it is not easy to talk about abuse. I wondered for a long time if it was my fault, but now I know it wasn't; I was an innocent child.

These stories are just a selected few from the many I received. I have chosen those stories which reflected the variety of ways in which children are abused and silenced. While they may be harrowing to read, don't lose sight of the fact that they did happen to real children of colour.

What is identifiable in all the stories is the undeniable fact that black children do feel they have been denied the right to tell and to ask for help to stop their pain. There wasn't one child who felt able to tell anyone else. This is also true for white children. The difference is that white children have white adults in supporting positions who can assist their healing and understand their pain both from a psychological and cultural point of view. Black children have to work hard at finding a black person in a similar position.

Many of the story-tellers acknowledge that they felt the abuse was a culturally exclusive activity. If black children can't feel free to identify their rights, we are failing them badly. How can people from different cultures begin to acknowledge and accept that so many black children are being abused when many black victims can't identify that for themselves? There is so much work to be done here.

Note

1 Patricia d'Ardenne and Aruna Mahtani, *Transcultural Counselling*. London: Sage, 1989.

CHAPTER 5
Case studies

In this chapter, I am going to invite you to use the information you have been offered so far in the book to assess for yourselves whether racism is easily identifiable. The two cases I will present are not real, but they very easily could be. They are in fact compilations of situations I have had firsthand experience of over the years of working in the area of child abuse.

Before we begin, there are some people I would like to introduce you to, and some information which may be useful to you. If there is suspicion of abuse, the situation has to be investigated, and one of the aspects of that investigation might well be a case conference. At a case conference, all interested parties are invited to attend to either report their suspicions, voice their concerns or just listen. A case conference is an opportunity for everyone to make a reasoned, rational decision with regard to a child's future welfare.

Some of the people invited to a case conference might include the following:

Social worker (Team leader and key worker)
Teacher(s)
Education welfare officer
Educational specialist (speech therapist, play therapist, nursery
    nurse, etc.) if any is working with the child(ren)
Health visitor
Police representative
Eduational psychologist
Legal representative
School medical officer
Parents and their support
Child(ren)
Chairperson
Minute-taker

Not all of these people are necessarily in the room at the same time;

for example, the parents may be invited to leave at some point so that issues of confidentiality which do not directly affect them are discussed.

A case conference can only recommend certain actions, it cannot necessarily enforce those actions. In most situations, however, the recommended course of action is taken. Some of the recommendations might include the following:

- That no further action be taken.
- That social worker involvement would be useful.
- That support and monitoring of the situation is necessary.
- That respite care be offered. (this sometimes means that the child(ren) may be accommodated by the local authority in a supportive environment if the parents need a rest. This is not the same as the local authority taking the child into care. Accommodation is much more a partnership between the local authority and the parents.)
- An interim care order (this is usually carried out when there is any real doubt as to the child(ren)'s safety and welfare if they were to continue living at home).
- Child(ren) may be placed on the Child Protection Register. (This usually means that there is some concern about the welfare of the child(ren) and, in all parties' interests, there will be regular updating of information and a key worker will be appointed to work closely with the family.)

According to the Children Act 1989,[1] each local authority has a duty to take the following points into consideration:

- A child's race, culture and religion, particularly when there is concern about the child's welfare. At all times, the child's welfare is of paramount importance.
- Each child is entitled to protection from neglect, abuse and exploitation.
- Each child's family life may vary, but if it meets the child's needs, it should be respected.
- Harm means ill-treatment, or the impairment of health and development.
- Where there is a question of whether harm suffered by a child is significant, rests on the child's health and development and how that compares to what could reasonably be expected of a similar child from a similar cultural and ethnic background.

CASE STUDY

Case Study One: Leon

Leon is a 3-year-old child from a Caribbean family background. His father is a musician and spends most of his time away from home, coming back at unexpected moments and disappearing again just as quickly. His mother has two other children who are older than Leon; one girl is 10 and the other is 8. The mother works as a supervisor in a large chain store. She is working her way up the promotional ladder and often has to attend evening training sessions. She always keeps her weekends free for the children. When the mother is working, she employs a babysitter, the 16-year-old daughter of a family friend. Both sets of grandparents live in the Caribbean. During the day, Leon attends a local private nursery on a full-time basis, which means he is out of the home from 8.45 a.m. to 5.30 p.m. During the day at the nursery, he is given ample opportunity to sleep and rest and he has a good appetite. The parents don't see much of each other, but it seems to suit them. There is certainly no rancour between them. The children do appear to be somewhat affected by their father's fleeting visits, Leon possibly more than his older sisters, who are becoming used to this state of affairs. Over the past few months the father has been home more often, and although he still goes out most nights, he is there in the evenings. Mother is having a very busy, demanding time at work and is being considered for the position of Head Supervisor. She is working until 10 p.m. most nights. By the time she comes home, the children have been put to bed by the babysitter, who often has a friend round to help her.

INCIDENT

When Leon was dropped off at the nursery by his mother, she mentioned that he hadn't been sleeping well and had been waking in the middle of the night and crying. He had been given a dose of paediatric medication in case he had a pain and put back to bed. He eventually went back to sleep but was restless for the remainder of the night. She said that if he didn't appear to be well, the nursery should contact her or the father, who should be at home. During the course of the day, Leon became withdrawn. He wet his pants on two occasions, which was very unusual for him. He hit out at two little girls who had previously been good friends with him. When it was the usual time for a rest period, Leon became quite agitated. He wouldn't lie down and screamed if anyone attempted to cover him with the sheet. When one of the nursery nurses tried to give him a cuddle, he kicked out at her and bit her hard on the left breast as she held him to her. The head-teacher called Leon's father who had just woken up and told him to come and collect his son as he was becoming uncontrollable. By the time his father arrived, Leon was calmer, but his father wasn't. He walked into the nursery and grabbed his son, who began to scream again. When the headteacher remonstrated with Leon's father for behaving so aggressively, she was told to mind her own business and that if she had given Leon a beating when he began playing up, there wouldn't have been any need to call him out. The following day when Leon's mother brought him to nursery, there was a social worker waiting to speak to her with regard to the nursery's concern about her husband's treatment of their son. The social worker asked the mother's permission to take Leon to a doctor for a physical examination. While this upset her, she agreed to the examination, provided she was present in the room. During the examination, the doctor noticed some old bruising around Leon's buttocks which gave him some concern. Leon was distressed about being examined and took a long time to calm down. When the nurse came into the room to help him get dressed, he began screaming again and tried to hide behind his mother. The social worker told the mother that there was some concern about Leon's welfare and that he would be calling a meeting to discuss with other relevant people what should be done. It would also mean that if abuse was suspected, Leon might be interviewed by a police officer and a social worker. His mother was advised to seek legal advice.

THE STATEMENTS

'My name is Mrs Clark. I am Leon's nursery teacher. I was trained in secondary education, but I found that I had diffi-culty controlling the older children, they were so boisterous, they frightened me, particularly the coloured boys who were quite insolent. I felt that my skills would be best suited to the little ones, who just need love and cuddles. They enjoy playing so there's not much to do. I make a point of treating all the children the same. I won't tolerate unfairness. Some of the parents don't speak English very well, but if I just smile at them and talk very slowly and loudly, they seem to understand. Using simple language really helps, because they're just like children really, aren't they? I like to have the children come to sit on my knee when I'm telling a story. Leon used to enjoy sitting on my knee and I learned some interesting things about his family. He once told me that his mother plaits his sisters' hair when they are asleep. I love his imagination. He's very bright for his age. I've stopped letting him sit on my knee now, because he used to get a bit rude. He would try to touch my chest or pinch me. He gets a bit over-excitable sometimes too and wants to kiss me on my mouth. I don't allow that. Recently Leon has been more naughty than he usually is. All the little coloured boys are lively but that's just their way. But there have been times when he has started to bite the little girls and I even found him lying on top of one the other day. He's becoming a bit of a bully. I'm a little bit frightened of him now, you just never know with this type of child do you?'

'I am Nicole. I am a qualified nursery nurse and have worked at the nursery for six months. I work in Mrs Clark's room. I have been concerned about Leon for some time now. When I first came to the school, he was a happy, outgoing little boy. He had many friends among the children in the class and played contentedly with them. I've met his mother just to say hello and goodbye to when she leaves Leon and then collects him. He is always pleased to see her and she is very loving towards him. But recently she has been in much more of a hurry, as she has had to get back to work again in the evenings for some training. Sometimes his father would collect him. He's a tall man, very lively, not as affectionate as his wife. He seems to expect more disciplined behaviour from Leon. I think he feels a bit uncomfortable coming to the nursery. Sometimes the girl who babysits comes to collect him and he plays up dreadfully. I wonder if he resents the fact that his mother couldn't come. I have been observing Leon's behaviour over the past few weeks, because there appeared to be a change in his personality. He has wet himself a few times which is surprising, as he has been toilet trained for a long while now. He spends a lot of time on his own, sitting with one toy, not even playing with it all the time, just staring into space. Usually he enjoys drawing and painting. He mostly paints the family. Recently, however, he has been painting pictures and then spoiling them by covering them with dark colours like brown or black. He also seems more angry than before. He throws things, and spends more and more time under a table in the hallway which has a cloth hanging down over it. If he ever goes missing we can usually guarantee he is there. When we had small doll-play one day, Leon got quite involved. He kept calling the little boy doll naughty and smacked it many times. I asked him why the doll was naughty, but he just mumbled. I've also noticed that he is much more interested in the little girls, especially at toilet time. He really stares at them. He's been caught pulling their panties down on a couple of occasions. The thing that concerns me most about Leon is that he doesn't appear to be happy any more. He loses his temper very quickly, and becomes overpoweringly violent. The other day I tried to comfort him and he bit me on my breast and left a mark.'

'I am Miss Watson, headteacher of the nursery that Leon attends. I don't usually have much direct contact with parents during the normal course of the day, but I do know them all and have spoken to them on several occasions. I was informed by the class teacher that Leon's mother had said if he appeared ill, then to either call her at work or her husband at home to collect the child. During the normal rest period which happens after lunch, Leon refused to take a nap and became violent, even biting Nicole when she tried to comfort him. I called his father, who told me he had just woken up. I insisted he come to collect his child, as by now he was uncontrollable. When he eventually arrived, he didn't stop to introduce himself but marched straight into the class and grabbed Leon by the arm. The child was very upset. I tried to explain to Mr —— that we don't use that sort of behaviour here, but he was very rude to me. He told me to beat his child. I was shocked. He is such a big man that I was quite concerned for my own safety. I felt that I could do no more than contact the Social Services department for advice. I cannot allow men to physically abuse their children no matter what colour they are.'

'I am the social worker. I was called to the nursery by the headteacher, who believed that one of the children was being abused by his father. I was at the school when the child arrived with his mother. I explained that there was some concern about her child's welfare and requested that she give her permission to have a doctor examine her child. She agreed. At the surgery, the doctor found some old bruising on the buttocks. The mother couldn't offer an explanation for them. The child appeared to be in good health. He was rather uncommunicative, but that was to be expected under the circumstances. The only time he demonstrated any temper was when the nurse came to give assistance. He became very agitated and eventually the mother asked that the nurse leave the room. Once this happened, the child calmed down. The doctor was concerned about the child's demeanour and the unexplained marks. I visited the parents at home and explained to the father the purpose of my visit. I was not there to point the finger of blame, but I did have the child's welfare as a priority and as such, I needed to ask some questions. I was offered a police escort but I didn't see why I should need one. I asked the father to explain what he meant by beating the child. He said it was just a smack and that all Caribbean children are raised strictly. The mother supported his statement and told me that as his father was hardly ever at home, the discipline was left to her. When any of the children misbehaved they were punished. I accepted this explanation, but said that I felt it might be necessary to clear up the matter with a case conference, as there clearly were some marks on their child and his behaviour was bizarre. I was also able to tell them that as a matter of course, Leon would be interviewed by trained personnel. The parents were invited to bring him along, but they wouldn't necessarily both be allowed to stay in the interview room. They were agreeable to this. The father appeared angry but calm. The mother was tearful.'

'I am the doctor who was asked to examine Leon. He was a well-developed boy, well within the height and weight percentiles for age. I cannot make a comment on language development as he was silent throughout, apart from becoming tearful and distressed when my nurse offered to assist in his dressing. There were several old bruises on his legs, which are very much in keeping with normal play rough and tumble. The marks on the child's buttocks, however, are much more of a concern. Unfortunately because he has dark skin, the imprint is less noticeable. However, it is old bruising, and while I would be reluctant to say so under oath, it has the appearance of a human adult bite mark. I would certainly recommend that the child's welfare be monitored. I am also the family GP. There is nothing outstanding in terms of health concerns in the family. No suspicious injuries in the past. The health visitor reports the usual developmental checks and routine vaccinations. The mother was always a regular attender at the baby clinic.'

'I am Lydia Glen. I am a social worker on the child protection team. I interviewed Leon. The interview was videoed by a colleague from the police. Leon was asked which parent he wanted to stay with him in the room. He chose his mother. I had already given instructions to both parents that when I began the interview, they had to be silent. Their presence was to reassure their child, not to take part. In the interview room were some toys such as Lego, some dolls and a puppet. At first Leon wandered round the room touching nothing. His mother and I sat on chairs until he was more used to me. I was selected for this interview as I am also Caribbean and it was considered that it might help the family by seeing someone from a familiar culture. Leon picked up some Lego and began to build. I asked if I could join in; he nodded. We made a house. I asked him who lives in the house; he said a bad boy. I asked him who the bad boy was. He shook his head. He picked up a large doll and threw it on the floor. He then found a male doll from a small world family (miniature dolls) and put it inside the house. He piled Lego bricks on top of the doll. I asked him if that was the bad boy. He nodded. I asked him if the bad boy was him. He nodded. I asked him who told him he was a bad boy. He shook his head. He left the Lego and moved to another part of the room. He started to play with the puppet. I pretended that I thought the puppet was real and began to talk to it. I asked the puppet if it knew Leon. It nodded. I asked it if Leon was really a bad boy. The puppet nodded again. I asked the puppet what bad boys did. After a period of silence the "puppet" said, "They turn me on". I asked the puppet how did that make a boy bad. The "puppet" replied, "Bad boys are dirty boys". I asked the puppet who says Leon is a bad boy, but the puppet was taken off his hand and Leon told me, "It's gone to sleep now".

'We had been in the interview room for over thirty minutes and I felt that was enough for one session.

'I now have concerns that this child may be being sexually abused and strongly suggest that more investigation is carried out. The mother has agreed to take leave from work, at least until after the case conference.'

'I am Leon's mother. I am frightened by what is happening to my son. I cannot understand how anyone could have abused him because he is always with an adult. I know my husband is much more of a disciplinarian than me, especially with Leon as the boy, but I know he loves him. Leon loves his daddy too. I have noticed that Leon has been a bit quiet recently, but I thought he must be starting with chicken-pox or something. There's a lot going round in the nursery. He's been a bit of a mummy's boy lately, always wanting to stay with me and crying when I leave him at the nursery. In fact I wondered if something was happening there, as he was coming home so bad-tempered. I asked the teacher, but she said everything was fine. When I've been home in time to give him his bath, he's been most odd. He asked me to kiss his willy. I was really angry with him. I told him that it was rude and not to say such things. I don't know where he hears such rubbish. He even tried to touch my breasts. I really smacked him for that.

'I assumed this was another phase he was going through. I've had two girls so I wasn't sure how boys behaved. These rages are getting worse, although since I've taken some time off to be with him up to the case conference, he's been a lot quieter. Cindy, my friend's daughter, says she misses coming round. I think she misses the money as well. I asked Leon if he wanted to go to Cindy's house, but he said no. He doesn't want to go to nursery any more either. I feel really guilty that I didn't spend more time with him. I am scared they'll take him away from me. Maybe they think I'm a bad mother.'

'I'm Leon's father. I spend a lot of time away from home working. I am a musician. I think children should be given discipline. It never harmed me. My wife is too soft sometimes. I had only just got out of bed when the school called. I was still half asleep. I had been working till 4 a.m. in a local club. They told me to come and get him straight away, that he was going berserk. I don't know why they didn't give him a beating there and then. Women aren't firm enough. By the time I got to the school I was mad. I wasn't going to waste time being polite, I wanted to get my kid and go. This headteacher told me that she didn't like the way I handled my son. What business is it of hers anyhow? I don't tell her how to handle her teachers. I might have been a bit rude, but she was rude to me. She acted as if she was scared of me. She kept saying things like, "Your kind of people". I didn't know what the woman was talking about. If I have to, I discipline my kids. Leon is a boy so he needs to be tough. I'm not going to let them change him into a sissy.'

There is no police record on Leon's father.

That is the information which was available during the case conference.

If you were the chairperson, what questions would you need to ask which would assist either in coming to a decision, or throwing more light on to the problem? Were you aware of any racist stereotyping? What would you recommend? Do you believe that Leon has been abused? if so, by whom?

I think we'll let Leon tell his story.

'I am Leon. I'm a big boy now. I'm 3. My mummy works in a big shop and sometimes I go to see her with my daddy. My big sisters come too. Daddy plays music. He can't sing though. I can sing. I can sing "Happy Birthday". Sometimes there is a bad boy. Bad boys "turn me on". Bad boys "make me real dirty". Bad boys get punished. Am I a bad boy? Mummy said I'm a bad boy. She smacked me. Mrs Clark knows I'm a bad boy. She won't let me sit on her knee any more. Nicole knows I'm a bad boy. Sometimes I get so mad! I bite and bite. I'm a bad black boy. Boys are bad. Black boys are worse. They like it. "Ooh, he's so big. He turns me on." Cindy says I'm a good boy. Cindy's friend says I'm a bad black boy. She says she's going to hurt my mummy. She says she can 'cos she's smart. Cindy says "stop", but her friend says, "he likes it". One day she said I was a bad black boy in the bath and hurt my botty. She bited me. Cindy says "stop", but her friend say, "It won't show". I cried for mummy but she said she would send mummy away. I like mummy being home. I like daddy being home. I don't like Cindy any more.'

Some clues as to how Leon was feeling came through his behaviour. His rages tended to be directed against white females. He had been terrified into silence. The fear of being responsible for the death of a parent can keep anyone quiet. What couldn't be silenced was the confusion. It came out as temper, it came out as nightmares, it came through Leon attempting to act out the incidents of abuse, by trying the same touches he had been encouraged to use on the abusive person, on those he trusted: his mother, his nursery nurse, his teacher. All three women unwittingly gave him the response that the abuser had promised bad boys would get: rejection. For a child who has been inappropriately sexualized by an adult, the behaviour they exhibit is bizarre, sexy and threatening. There appears to be no consistency, no reason for the anger. There are many stories of this type of abuse. When this is linked to the colour of a child's skin, there is even more damage. Leon may consider that being black is bad. Only white people are good. White females should become objects of hate, and so on. Fortunately for Leon his dilemma was noted, the abuse stopped and he and his family were offered therapy to overcome the problems.

There were some basic misunderstandings caused by the ignorance of the staff looking after Leon. For example, to 'beat' a child means to smack. It has a different connotation to a white-English meaning. While it may be seen to be undesirable from a professional's point of view, there are many families, including those from a Caribbean background, who still feel that good discipline which includes beatings/smacks is acceptable. The children are raised to respect the adults, understanding that it is the parents' love for their children which necessitates this action. Those of us who were raised within a Christian environment would have certainly heard the adage: 'Spare the rod and spoil the child.' This would often be accompanied by the statement: 'This hurts me more than it hurts you.' Bearing this in mind, it would have been useful for the school to give each prospective parent a brochure outlining the school's policy on equality of opportunity for children, the methods of discipline within the school and the attitudes towards punishment, including the rationale behind those views. There could have been stated recognition of the important role of the parents in the education of their children, etc. If there had been an opportunity for parents and staff to discuss the expectations which each have of the other, then perhaps terms for different aspects of discipline could have been discussed, alongside differing styles of parenting, the value of a partnership with the parents so that they present a united front for their children, and so on.

It would also be vital for the staff to constantly update their awareness of anti-discrimination practice. Why was there an undercurrent of fear about Leon's father? Perhaps the staff are still stuck in their own racism. There is an anxiety about an angry black man. There is still the acceptance that black African/Caribbean men have less control of their tempers and consequently are more likely to be physically restrained as a 'precaution' than a white or Asian male. We still see Caribbean cultures as being much more matriarchal, and again this can be detrimental. Perhaps the staff at the school had been sitting in judgement on Leon's mother spending so many hours working. Perhaps they felt she should have been spending more time with the boy.

It's often difficult to identify how racism permeates attitudes towards or against someone. For professionals working with children, it is essential that they constantly check out why they thought that; how they came to that conclusion; did they feel differently about certain parents based on skin colour, culture or religion? The important person in all of this is the child, and no one should forget to take that into account. Acknowledgement of the variety of child-rearing practices and parenting skills is essential. There has to be a line drawn between what is seen as different and what is seen as bad. How can that be identified? If there is any doubt, it is valuable to remember the welfare check-list given in the Introduction. I list it briefly here:

1 Does the child have a good standard of health (apart from the usual complaints of childhood)?
2 Does the child demonstrate development according to age range in the following areas:

- *physical* (skills, ability, growth);
- *intellectual* (demonstration of growing awareness of concepts, thought processes, the world around them);
- *language* (normal speech patterns, depending on whether the child is monolingual or multilingual, use of vocabulary and non-verbal communication);
- *emotional* (self-awareness, developing awareness of others, understanding and controlling feelings);
- *social* (contact with peers and adults, forming appropriate relationships, coping with changing relationships)?

3 Where the child has an acknowledged need – a physical disability, a learning disability, an emotional disability or a health

need – is development still apparent, however slow the rate?

Having a reference point often allays fears that a particular style of parenting is detrimental. If there are still concerns, these should be discussed with the parents of the child in an atmosphere of mutual respect and trust. For example, some people are concerned about children fasting during Ramadan.[2] If a child is unwell at the beginning of the fasting period, he or she will not be expected to fast. Muslim parents are very aware of their children's health needs.

CASE STUDY

Case Study Two: Sunita
Sunita is 5 years old. She is the youngest child in a family of four. Her mother and father came to this country from India in 1985. Her father works in a local factory as an engineer. Her mother stays at home. The other children are much older than Sunita and are either married or in secondary school. The paternal grandfather came to live with the family when his wife died last year. He has taken over some of the outside family duties, such as escorting Sunita to and from school, doing some of the main shopping and chaperoning the mother when she goes out. It is assumed by the school that Sunita's mother has very little English, as she never converses with anyone even when she comes to the school to collect her daughter. The family wear traditional dress and appear to be quite religious. The school is not sure which religion they practice, but it is either Hindu or Muslim. There are no problems at mealtimes as Sunita brings a packed lunch. The school has a policy of allowing children from different cultures to dress according to their tradition, so that even during physical education class, Sunita doesn't need to undress. Sunita has always been a quiet child. She gets on with her school work, not necessarily understanding everything, but never giving the teacher any cause to raise her voice. She smiles at adults quite freely, but speaks so softly that it is often difficult to catch what she is saying. Her father and grandfather are both similar in manner and appearance. Neither smiles easily and neither appears willing to spend time talking to the teachers about Sunita. The staff accept this as

part of the family's culture, as it appears that women have no real significance. While there may be times when it would have been useful to have had a chat about Sunita, it is accepted that this will not happen. In some ways it is a relief as both men, especially the grandfather, have an accent which makes listening to them and understanding them difficult. One of the classroom assistants once reported seeing Sunita's grandfather in the local supermarket pushing a trolley, and instead of saying 'Excuse me' in order to get past the shoppers, he clapped his hands and gestured for people to move. It caused some resentment at the time, as most of the shoppers were women. Over the past few months, Sunita has been looking quite dishevelled in the mornings. She is lethargic during playtime and spends most of it sitting on the wall. She hardly ever plays with her friends now, not even the ones from her own culture. This was observed by the support teacher, who comes in twice a week to work with those children who are a bit slower at reading, or who have English as a second language. She saw Sunita on one of these mornings and was concerned that she appeared unable to concentrate, nor was she willing to give answers to the comprehension questions. This was unusual, as she normally enjoyed her special time with that teacher. When she mentioned it to the class teacher, she was told that Sunita was still as well behaved in class, 'just a bit dim'. She would sit in front of the computer without actually doing anything until one of the other children pushed her away. The teacher didn't see that there was a problem.

DAY OF INCIDENT

All the children had taken letters home giving information about an outbreak of TB in the area and stating that, as a precautionary measure, all children from the school were being offered skin tests to see whether they needed additional protection. Those parents who agreed to this gave their consent for their children to be tested at the school. Those children whose parents wished to take them to their own doctors again had signatures to verify this. Sunita had no signature on her letter. The teacher waited until the parents came to collect their children and asked Sunita's grandfather if he or his son had read the letter and, if there was anything they didn't understand, she would explain it to him. He didn't appear to understand her, and when the teacher mentioned the word 'doctor' he became very agitated. He pushed Sunita out of the cloakroom and waved the teacher away with his hand.

For the rest of that week Sunita did not attend school. According to school policy, if a child has a prolonged period of absence without the parents giving a reason, the school automatically notifies the education welfare officer. This happened in Sunita's case. A letter was sent to the family home but nothing happened. Sunita did not return to school for another week. When she did come back, she was much thinner, subdued and looked quite ill. The teacher again attempted to talk to the grandfather but he refused to talk to her. He pushed Sunita roughly into the classroom and then left. In the afternoon he brought Sunita's mother along and she came in for the child.

There followed another period of prolonged absence. This time the education welfare officer went to the house. He was not invited in. He didn't see Sunita on that visit, but felt that there was enough concern now, with regard to the child's welfare, to contact social services. A social worker visited the school and spoke to the headteacher. A request was made to list concerns about the child, the main one obviously being her numerous absences. The social worker went to Sunita's, but couldn't get anyone to answer the door. She left a card to say when she had called and when she would return. When she returned a few days later, she was greeted at the door by the grandfather, who told her that Sunita had gone back to India. The social worker said she needed to talk to Sunita's parents before she could complete her report. She requested that the parents contact her to arrange a meeting.

When the social worker returned to the office, she made enquiries about whether there had been anything reported about this family in the past. Looking through the log-book for the previous month, she found two reports from neighbours about a child crying for a prolonged period of time. When this was followed up, the grandfather is reported to have said that his grandchild had toothache and that she was being taken to the dentist. There was also an unconfirmed report about a child seen out in the street late at night wearing very little clothing and appearing to have bare feet. The father contacted the social worker and expressed surprised that the grandfather had said Sunita was in India. She was at home. So far as he knew, Sunita had been attending school. The social worker took her concerns to her supervisor and it was agreed that a case conference should be held.

MINUTES OF CASE CONFERENCE ABOUT SUNITA S ——

Apologies: GP
                     Headteacher
Those present: Class teacher
                     Social worker
                     Health visitor
                     Support teacher
                     Parents
                     Interpreter for parents
                     Representative from police

There was also a letter from a neighbour who had reported her concerns about Sunita.

The chairperson begins:

'I would like to thank you for coming to this case conference about Sunita S____. What I propose is that each of the relevant people, in turn, give a report on their involvement with Sunita, and any observations and concerns they wish to state.'

'My name is Veronica Green. I am the class teacher. Sunita has been with me since she left the reception class in September. She has always been a quiet, well-behaved child. In fact I hardly know she's there. I can't tell you much about her as I am usually so busy working with the children who are rather more energetic. There are thirty children in my class. Over the past few months Sunita has been absent for many days. Out of a possible total of sixty full days, Sunita has only been in school for twenty-five. When I approached her grandfather to discuss this, he just ignored me. I brought this to the attention of the headteacher, who contacted the Education Welfare Department. While I did not see anything myself, it has been reported to me that sometimes Sunita behaves in a strange way, particularly towards the little boys. She has also been reported to have been more than usually reluctant to use the toilet. It is almost as if she doesn't want to go in there. My assistant says that Sunita has been quite tearful when she really needs to use the toilet and wondered if she had a pain. On one occasion, there appeared to be some blood in the toilet after she had used it, but it could easily have been tomatoes or something else that she ate. We don't see much of Sunita's mother now as her grandfather has taken on the task of bringing her to and from school. I don't think Sunita is happy with this arrangement, as she often looks quite tearful and almost frightened as she leaves. Sometimes I find her looking at me so intently I wonder what is going through her mind. Her grandfather is very protective of her. He doesn't even like her to talk to the other children when he is taking her home. I suppose that is their way. Since Sunita has come back from her last absence, I was quite shocked by her weight loss. It must have been a serious illness for her to lose so much weight. She is not as lively as she used to be and behaves almost as if she isn't always aware of her surroundings. I must confess to being rather impatient with Sunita as she speaks in such a quiet voice that it is frustrating, and if I ask her to speak up she becomes even more quiet. I would describe her progress as slow; she doesn't ask when she needs help, so therefore I am not always aware of what she can or cannot do. She muddles through. I feel that her grandfather is quite disrespectful to me as the teacher, but I think that's cultural. They don't have much time for women do they? I think this is all just a misunderstanding; maybe he's scared of Immigration coming and sending him back.'

'My name is Gill Dent. I am the support teacher at the school. I see those children who need additional support with reading skills and children who are bilingual like Sunita. I see Sunita once a week for about twenty minutes. She is a pleasant, bright child who blossoms in a smaller, more intimate environment, away from the noise and bustle of the classroom. She is Hindu. Her mother is a shy woman according to Sunita, who is self-conscious about her English. She has a stammer, which makes it difficult for her. Sunita was doing really well in my class up to the time that her grandfather came to stay. She subsequently became progressively anxious, not concentrating on her work and jumping every time I touched her or spoke to her. She said she was tired. There were some occasions when she appeared to be doubled up in pain, but wouldn't accept any comfort. There was one incident that stands out in my mind. Sunita had drawn a picture which looked like someone lying on the bed (a girl) and a man standing holding something in his hand. I asked her to tell me about the picture. She said that the girl had been bad and was going to be stabbed and cut open. She became quite excited about this and made stabbing motions with her clenched fist. That was unusual for her; she normally drew pictures of the family. I told her I didn't think that was a nice story to write about and for her to put the paper away. She screwed the paper up and put it in the bin. I was rather wary of her for a while after that but she just got on with things. Though I must remark that she never spoke to me about her family again. Sunita's work has deteriorated recently and I have concerns about her possibly requiring additional support. I saw Sunita out shopping with her grandfather the other day; she recognized me but lowered her head so that we didn't have to speak. This is out of character for her.'

'I am the health visitor for Dr _____. I have checked through the health records for Sunita and can see no major concerns. I understand she has had several absences from school, but she has not been to the doctor, apart from one occasion four months ago when her mother brought her in. She had torn the skin round her anal opening. The doctor thought she probably had thread worms and had been scratching too vigorously. He prescribed some medication and presumably it worked as she was never brought back.'

'My name is Ermine Jones. I am the social worker appointed to the S_____ family. I was contacted after concerns were expressed by the school and education welfare officer about Sunita's number of absences from school. I made arrangements to visit the family and on the first occasion could not gain access as everyone appeared to be out. I left a card stating when I would return. On that occasion I was greeted at the door by the grandfather of the child, who told me that Sunita had gone to India. After telling him that I needed to confirm this by talking to the parents, I again left my number for Mr or Mrs S_____ to contact me. Mr S _____ called and said that his daughter was at home and that he had no knowledge of his daughter's absence from school. He said I must have misunderstood his father: most people couldn't understand him. I ran a check to see if there was any further information about the family and discovered that there had been two complaints about a child crying and one report of a child being left outside in unsuitable clothing. There were no confirmations of the child being left outside, and the grandfather said Sunita had toothache. However, I have since received a letter from the same neighbour with photographs. I will read the letter. "I am writing to say how worried I am about a little girl who lives at the end of my street. My house joins on to hers and I can hear sounds quite clearly through my bedroom wall. There are many nights when I have heard her crying out and then the sound of a man's voice followed sometimes by the sound of a slap. This noise is usually about 2 a.m. I have sometimes gone downstairs and looked to see if the lights were on, but they never have been. When I have spoken to Mrs S _____ about it, she says she doesn't know what I mean. She is fast asleep and so are all the family. This noise has been going on for the last six months. During the very cold spell we had, I looked out of my window and I saw the little girl standing outside the back door with no shoes on her feet, crying. I called to her and her grandfather opened the door and dragged her in. I reported that to social services but I don't know if anything happened. The same thing has happened twice more. One of those times, I was so angry I took a photograph of the child and I enclose it for you. [Photograph shows Sunita crouching down outside door. There appears to be ice or frost on the ground. It is unclear whether she is wearing shoes.] I am sure that child is being treated badly. I know I sound like an interfering old woman, but I can't just sit and do nothing."

I am very concerned now for this child's safety and recommend that we investigate further.'

In the light of this information, an investigation was carried out by the police and social services. A full physical examination of Sunita revealed that she had been sexually interfered with. There were tears in her vagina and scar tissue round her anus. During the video interview, she disclosed that her grandfather had been abusing her since he had begun to share the same bedroom with her. The abuse involved touching, oral sex and penetration. He has since been arrested.

Part of the investigation involved interviewing both parents. These are their statements:

'I am Sunita's mother. She is a good girl, always helpful and well-behaved. We were a very happy family until my husband's father came to live with us. After a week of sleeping on the bed we made up for him in the spare bedroom, he claimed that he had a bad back and that he needed a wider bed than the single one. Sunita sleeps in a double bed and when we have some of our older children come to stay, she moves in with us. I said, all right, I would move Sunita out of her bed. He said, no, it didn't matter about her, she was so small she wouldn't take up too much room. I didn't feel happy about this but he was my father-in-law so what could I do? My husband seemed to think it was all right. After that he slept in Sunita's bed every night. I asked her if she minded but she said, no it was OK. But she has changed. She is not the happy child she used to be. She often cries now and says she has a pain in her tummy. She asks if she can come with me when I go out, but I say, no, you must go to school. I have a job now to help bring money into the house and my father-in-law says he will look after Sunita. I wonder if he can look after a little girl properly but he says he helped raise his own daughter so why should I worry? By the time I come home Sunita is usually tired, so when she cries I think that is why. There have been times when I thought I heard her cry out in the night, but when I go to see, my father-in-law says go back to bed, there is nothing wrong. I wish I had been braver, then my daughter wouldn't have been so badly hurt.'

'I am Sunita's father. I think you have all made a mistake, my father wouldn't do something like this to his own grandchild. He is a good man. He looked after us when my mother was ill. He was especially kind to my sisters. Some of them used to think it was a treat to share his bed. We don't abuse children in my culture. We love children. I refuse to believe what you are telling me. Sunita is lying. I will get her to tell you the truth. This can't be true.'

For a family like this one, there will be much pain and suffering. It is unlikely that Sunita's father will ever be able to accept what he has been told about his daughter's abuse. If that is the case, then he cannot be relied on to be her protector. The mother seems more able to believe this, probably because she is the daughter-in-law and not an actual daughter. It sounds as though Mr S____'s sisters might have experienced similar behaviour when they were younger. It may be possible to ask them, but it won't help the child.

Let's look at what has happened here. Why were things allowed to get so bad before something was done? These might be some of the reasons. The attitude of the staff gave cause for concern. They didn't know the culture and religion of the child. They had assumed that the male members of the family had little time for women, when Mr S ____ could possibly have been approachable. Instead they waited until there was a problem that someone else could deal with, i.e. the absence from school. When the support teacher voiced her concern, the class teacher basically ignored the suggestion that something might be wrong. The support teacher also failed to take note of the pictures which Sunita drew. Instead, she told her to get rid of them. When a child is given messages like that, it often blocks their motivation to tell another person. While it is not necessarily the teacher's job to be able to recognize every cry for help, more attention should have been paid to the fact that this was unusual behaviour for this particular child.

There appears to have been a refusal to see what was obvious on the part of most of the professionals dealing with this situation. This can be the case when no one will take responsibility for making the first move. The behaviour of the school staff indicated an avoidance of getting into lengthy discussions with the grand-father and previously, the mother, on the assumption that it would be too difficult to communicate. That is another form of racism. If someone appears unable to speak in an understandable way, let's ignore them and then we don't have to feel uncomfortable and exasperated. The same thing applied to Sunita's teacher. Sunita was pressurized to speak louder, when her reaction was to become quieter in order to demonstrate respect. I would follow that she also lowered her head when in the presence of a teacher, again showing respect. Bullying by white adults and children towards Asian adults and children is a very common form of racism. The affronted classroom assistant considered the behaviour of the grandfather to be rude when she saw him in the supermarket. Rudeness would have been to crash into people as a way of making them move. Throughout this, there was a gradual build-up of resistance against the family even before Sunita showed any signs of distress. This is not acceptable, and denies children access to support and protection.

It is possible that the doctor misdiagnosed Sunita's condition as threadworms, partly, we can guess, because he was not looking for any sign of abuse and perhaps because Sunita's mother made light of the child's condition as Sunita had given her no reason to think of anything untoward. Whether Dr _____ was too busy to attend the case conference or whether he felt there was nothing for him to report personally of any significance remains open to conjecture.

Notes

1   Children Act 1989, Section 17(1), London: HMSO, 1991.
2   A period of fasting during the ninth month on the Muslim calender, when the faithful fast during the hours of sunrise to sunset. It is an opportunity to experience deprivation. In some Muslim communities, children begin fasting when they are 9 years old. In other communities, girls are expected to fast at an earlier age than boys. It teaches self-discipline and self-awareness. At the end of the month there is a celebration called Eid al Fitr, where everyone shares their food and gives gifts to friends, relatives and neighbours.

CHAPTER 6
Statistics

I have a problem with statistics. Although I am about to offer some to you, I cannot swear to feel necessarily good about that. When I was completing my first degree, one of the books for recommended reading was *How to Lie with Statistics* by Darrell Huff, from which the following extract is taken:

> The secret language of statistics, so appealing in a fact-minded culture, is employed to sensationalize, inflate, confuse and over-simplify. Statistical methods and statistical terms are necessary in reporting the mass data of social and economic trends, business conditions, 'opinion' polls, the census. But without writers who use the words with honesty and understanding and readers who know what they mean, the result can only be semantic nonsense.
>
> In popular writing on scientific matters the abused statistic is almost crowding out the picture of the white-jacketed hero labouring overtime without time-and-a-half in an ill-lit labora-tory. Like the 'little dash of powder, little pot of paint', statistics are making many an important fact 'look like what she ain't'. A well-wrapped statistic is better than Hitler's 'big lie'; it misleads, yet it cannot be pinned on you.[1]

This has been a contributory factor in my cynicism. When politi-cians present 'factual' figures, whether they concern unemployment, employment, immigrants, senior citizens, and so on, I am amazed at the wealth of 'realistic' evidence they churn out. I thus found it all the more puzzling when I began to make enquiries of various statu-tory and voluntary bodies about their statistics with regard to the number of black children on child abuse registers, the number of black children who are considered at risk and the number of black children who have actually been at risk from potential abuse, to be informed by most of these organizations that they do not keep figures of that kind. To quote a Scotland Yard source: 'A child is a child, so it doesn't matter what colour they are.'[2] Unfortunately it does matter: to the child and to the child's family. This, I feel, is part of the conspiracy of silence which prevents black children from receiving the support, advice and recognition which is appropriate to their culture, their colour and their family system. However, we'll see where we get with the statistics I have managed to obtain. My intention in sharing the next few pages' worth of numbers with you is to highlight how difficult it can be to gain a really clear picture of the incidence of child abuse within the black population, the type of abuse within the black population and the abusers of children from within the black population. To try to make some sense of these numbers, let's begin with some simple facts. In 1991, there were thirteen million children in the United Kingdom (i.e. under the age of 18).[3] Of these,

- 98,000 had been reported as missing.
- 375,000 were registered as disabled.
- 60,500 were in public care.
- 48,000 were on the Child Protection Register.

After 1991, the criteria and terminology relating to the Child Protection Register changed because of the Children Act and other categories that were introduced. For example, 'grave concern' about a child was considered not specific enough, so children were eventually re-registered under more specific headings, such as 'at risk of sexual abuse', 'at risk of neglect', etc.

For a child to be considered as a candidate for the Child Protection Register, the case conference must decide whether there is the likelihood of harm leading to the need for child protection. One or other of the following requirements needs to be acknowledged:

1) There must be one or more identifiable incidents which can be described as having adversely affected the child. They may be acts of commission or omission. They can be either physical, sexual, emotional or neglect. It is important to identify a specific occasion or occasions when the incident(s) occurred. Professional judgement is that further incidents are likely; or
2) Significant harm is expected on the basis of professional judgement on findings of the investigation in this individual case or on research evidence.[4]

By March 1994,

- 34,900 children were on the Child Protection Register.
- In the age range of 10 and upwards, 57 per cent were girls. The total of girls of all ages worked out to 55 per cent.
- 69 per cent of the total number of children registered were under the age of 10.
- 62 per cent of the children registered under the category, sexual abuse, were girls.[5]

If we look at those figures, particularly those for children on the Child Protection Register and those in care, it is acceptable to assume that a sizeable percentage of those children were or had been in danger or being sexually abused, and that a fair percentage of those children would be black. In Chapter 1 mentioned the concern of the Muslim population about the lack of local authority awareness of the number of Muslim children in their care. While black as a colour cannot easily be overlooked or ignored, the culture of those children does not seem to warrant the same acknowledgement. In the London Borough of Newham, for example, the number of children on the Child Protection Register at any one time can range from 180 to 200.[6] Of those, when last reported (in 1995) around 47 per cent of the children were from black and minority ethnic backgrounds. There is a consistent over-representation of African children and an under-representation of Asian children. Does this mean that all cultures and religions of children are catered for? In Newham, that would appear to be the case, but could the same be said for every part of the country? Is there concern, for example, for African children which prompts the placing of such children on the Child Protection Register, which is not shown to the same degree for Asian children? Is there something about the way we view children and families from these ethnic groups which causes this apparent discrepancy? I know that Newham as a borough is working extremely hard to make itself a 'child-safe place', I know the staff receive race equality training, etc. So I wonder what happens?

How do figures for the incidence of child abuse from within certain ethnic groups compare in other parts of the world? Gail Wyatt found that in a survey carried out randomly on women from white backgrounds and African-American backgrounds, there was an equal incidence of childhood abuse which came out statistically as 1 in 2.5 African-American women and 1 in 2 white-American women who had experienced abuse during childhood.[7]

Professor Diana Russell in Oakland, California, came to a similar conclusion.[8] Her survey on randomly selected women from African-

American, Filipino, Asian, Latino and white-American back-grounds showed that a similar percentage in each group had been abused during childhood. In Britain, between 1989 and 1990, Southall Black Women's Centre had twenty-two enquiries involving sexual harassment, among which were nine cases of rape or incest.

In a comparative American survey produced in 1989, Hampton *et al.*[9] asked the question: 'Is violence in Black families increasing?' The general findings indicated that there was an increase in cases of child abuse linked to violence against black children of 26.8 per cent of all recorded cases. The authors noted that there was also an increase in the incidence of violence by black women towards black men. One of the theories they put forward to explain this trend is that the majority of families below the poverty line are from minority groups, a large proportion of whom will be black. There has been a rise in the number of better-educated black women marrying men on low incomes and with fewer academic qualifications and the inference is that the women are beating their men, who in turn take out their anger on their children. The survey also highlighted the fact that the number of battered black and white women was about equal.

Coley and Beckett,[10] again in America, in their research into the lack of equal numbers of black women using the facilities available to battered women, decided that most black women either didn't know about shelters or considered them to be predominantly for white women. In effect, they didn't think there was anywhere for them to go. This may also be the case for black children. Up until recent months, most of the public advertising for charitable support agencies has portrayed white children. Perhaps black children feel abandoned in the same way? The other points for consideration raised by the researchers were that black women tended to seek medical help first before counselling or psychological support. There was a tendency among workers to consider that black women were tough enough to withstand any amount of emotional battering, or the converse, that they are not psychologically sophisticated enough to have rational thought. The final consideration was that, somehow, black women may have experienced what was referred to as a 'trap of loyalty'. They could not disclose their problems in a culturally integrated setting without feeling the guilt of disloyalty to their own culture and racial group. I think it is apt to draw parallels here between the behaviour of black battered women and abused black children. If it is not made clear by society that all facilities with regard to shelter, support and protection are available to all people regardless of colour or culture, then the predominant group will almost always monopolize those services.

How are you doing so far?

If we look at information about the type of abuse suffered, again there is a problem with regard to statistics. It really depends on how the information is gathered. For example, some information comes straight from crime statistics, which basically means a crime of sexual abuse has been found to be serious enough to have been taken to court. These figures are among the lowest, as most cases of child abuse either don't get to court for one reason or another, or the perpetrator pleads quilty to a lesser charge. For example, in 1984, the actual number of proceedings against charges of unlawful intercourse with female children under the age of 13 was 115.[11] Those which went forward to trial at Crown Court amounted to seventy-three.

We then have incidents of child abuse reported to various agencies such as the NSPCC and ChildLine. Not all of these cases get to court, some are never proved, and some could be the number of actual incidents of abuse as opposed to the number of victims of abuse. Other figures are gained from a random selection formula. The two surveys carried out by Wyatt and Russell are both random. Mrazek *et al.* polled health professionals to ascertain how many sexually abused children they had come into contact with in a particular year.[12] The number is less important than how it was achieved. There would not have been a 100 per cent response rate; in fact, only 39 per cent of the health professionals responded. That means it is not a representative sample.

Surveys have been carried out by popular magazines which target readers of particular age groups. These give some indication of the faceless numbers of victims who survived childhood abuse despite never reporting the incidents or getting professional support, usually after the abuse has stopped. There is other research which looks at specific aspects of child abuse, possibly the gender of victims and/or perpetrators. Finklehor *et al.* conducted a survey which looked at what victims considered to be abuse, who victimized them, the predisposing factors to abuse, whether the child came from a dysfunctional family, whether both parents were still supporting the child, etc. The final aspect of the research was to identify the geographical region the victims came from or lived in. The conclusion of this particular research was that a history of sexual abuse can be found in the backgrounds of victims. Many victims never disclosed their abuse. Those children most at risk appeared to be those whose parents had separated, or where one parent was in poor health or had died. Two intriguing findings were that there was a disproportionate number of victims from the Pacific Coast and the incidence of child abuse seemed to be highest for those born between 1936 to 1946.[13]

So, those are some of the statistics. Where does that leave us in understanding why children are abused or why racism is an integral part of the experience of the black abused child? The answer is, it doesn't help one little bit. What it does is let us know that research is still being carried out in the hope that someone somewhere will find a solution.

Notes

1 Darrell Huff, *How to Lie with Statistics*. London: Pelican, 1975, p. 63.
2 While researching for factual information to include in this book, I telephoned, among other organizations, Scotland Yard for any statistics relating to the ethnic or cultural origin of children who had been sexually abused or raped. This was their response.
3 Children Act Training Day, 1993.
4 *Working Together under the Children Act 1989*, Department of Health. London: HMSO, 1991. The types of abuse listed in this document are: neglect; physical injury; sexual abuse, and emotional abuse. Categories of abuse for registration are:

  • neglect, physical injury and physical abuse
  • neglect and physical injury
  • neglect and sexual abuse
  • physical injury and sexual abuse
  • neglect (alone)
  • physical injury (alone)
  • sexual abuse (alone)
  • emotional abuse (alone)
  • categories not recommended by *Working Together* (1991)

5 Department of Health and Social Security, *Children and Young People on Child Protection Registers, Year Ending 31 March 1994*. London: HMSO, 1994. New statistics recently published for 1994 to March 1995 reveal that the number of children on the Child Protection Register in England is now 30,444. This may be due either to deregistration or to the new preventive measures adopted by many local authorities throughout the country.
6 A written reply from the head of child protection in Newham, Bernadette Manning, in response to a letter I circulated to all London boroughs, reads as follows:

The number of children on our register ranges from 180–200 at any one time. The ethnic breakdown reflects that of the Borough's population, about 47% of the children on the register are from black and minority ethnic backgrounds. We consistently have an over representation of African children and an under representation of Asian children.

The Borough has an interpreting service and our social work staff are of mixed racial backgrounds. There are no specific services for children from black or minority ethnic backgrounds.

Our staff do receive race equality training and it is a requirement that all staff training takes into account the cultural and religious backgrounds of the children with whom we work.

7 G.E. Wyatt, 'The sexual abuse of Afro-American and white American women in childhood'. *Child Abuse and Neglect*, **9** (1985), p. 65.

8 D. Russell, *The Secret Trauma. Incest in the Lives of Girls and Women*. New York: Basic Books, 1986.

9 R.I. Hampton, Gelles and Harrop, 'Is violence in black families increasing? A comparison of 1975 and 1985 national survey rates'. *Journal of Marriage and the Family*, **51** (November 1989), p. 66.

10 S.M. Coley and J.O. Beckett, 'Black battered women: practical issues'. *Social Casework: The Journal of Contemporary Social Work* (1988) (Family Service America).

11 Home Office, *Criminal Statistics. England and Wales: Statistics Relating to Crime and Criminal Proceedings*. London: HMSO, 1984.

12 P.J. Mrazek, Lynch and Bentovim, 'Sexual abuse of children in the United Kingdom'. *Child Abuse and Neglect*, **7** (1983), p. 67.

13 D. Finklehor, Hotaling, Lewis and Smith, 'Sexual abuse in a national survey of adult men and women: prevalence, characteristics and risk factors'. *Child Abuse and Neglect*, **14** (1990), p. 68.

CHAPTER 7
Mending hearts and broken promises

All children need to develop self confidence and a sense of self worth, so alongside the development of identity, and equally important, is self esteem. The questions 'Who am I?' and 'How do I feel about myself?' continue throughout life, but are particularly prominent during adolescence. Identity develops from knowledge and from understanding of one's place in the scheme of things, while self esteem is largely based on the perceived reactions of other people. Those who feel unloved, unwanted, belittled or discriminated against, will have their self esteem undermined.[1]

This final chapter is my opportunity to say what I think should be done to amend the insult to the black abused child. When I began to write this book, I had a clear idea of what I wanted to achieve. I wanted to write a book on a subject I felt strongly about in a way that wasn't overly threatening and negative. My purpose was to persuade by use of rational logic. Whether this is successful remains to be seen.

Let's begin with an essential issue: professionals and professional practice. People like me. What can we do? How can we offer the best support to the abused black child and his or her family? Clearly, there has to be more anti-discriminatory training on both a personal and professional level. It has to mean something more than just the occasional update. Anti-discriminatory awareness training should not be optional for those who will be working with people from different backgrounds and belief systems or, more specifically, those who are caring professionals, or those training the would-be caring professionals. When I first began my professional training back in the 1960s there were no such facilities available, and stereotyping was a way of life. I was raised in an area where there was no one from any other culture, except for the trainee doctors at the local teaching hospital, who stayed for a few years and then left for either more populated areas or to return to their South Asian roots. The information I gleaned about other people came straight out of books, with all their prejudices and bias. Because I read it, I believed it. I read that black people were always happy and I believed it, especially of 'our Commonwealth cousins'. I loved my books about Little Black Sambo. He was brave. He lived in the jungle. He was a caricature. I believed that black men couldn't keep up the pace of work achieved by white people because they were inherently lazy. I believed that emancipation of slaves meant freedom. Around me were adults who were physically revolted by black skin. Black people were called savages, and while I argued against it, I argued more out of sympathy for the underdog than to put forward a rational argument. At college I learned not to expect the same high standard of work from the black children. I disagreed with arranged marriages and couldn't understand that others may see this as the greatest form of love parents can show their children.

I moved to London in 1983, much older, more cynical perhaps, but all the better for that. I began to take more notice of the people I was working alongside and the students I was teaching. I preached tolerance and treating all children the same. I was given the opportunity to attend racial awareness sessions which was an optional training for the staff of the college where I worked. From a staff of over three hundred, five people attended. I experienced anger at being brought face to face with my racist beliefs. I resented the fact that the things I had believed with a 'charitable heart' were unfair, cruel assumptions made through an ignorance I had to work hard to overcome. I moved from racial awareness to anti-racism. I continued to train and retrain. The pain for me is that every time I either run anti-racist workshops or attend other anti-discriminatory sessions, I find something else I have to rethink. I will continue to do this, not because I am now so self-righteous, but because I still have a long way to go. Personal development must be the first duty of the professional carer, the motivation to want to change the *status quo* for the children who rely on us. There is an arrogant assumption among some of us who are in positions of power in the training of professional carers that we somehow don't need to do this work on ourselves any more. If those who directly influence the standards of professional practice cannot be bothered to be self-challenging, it does not bode well for the trainees. Beyond the development of a personal anti-racist strategy, there should be compulsory cultural awareness training to ensure that each child is properly recognized as the product of his or her own ethnic and cultural background. Look at Figure 7.1: What do you see? How many different pictures can you perceive? Which is the strongest image for you? When you hear about abused chlidren, what images do you have? If we add the colour black to that recipe, does that change the way you view the situation? Your response will depend on your history, whether you experienced abuse as a child, your cultural and ethnic identity, your role within your family group, your colour.

Figure 7.1

In a paper written in 1989, F.M. Hooper outlines the management of child abuse in the Zulu community of Natal[2]. The first problems encountered were connected to belief systems of the population: 'The Zulu's way of life as such did not lend itself, so it was believed, to the precipitation of child abuse.' He goes on to quote statistics which were beginning to prove that this view was false, but

the population at large as well as many professionals already involved in the field of child abuse still retained the rather naive view, that 'black people don't abuse their children – they love their children'.

It is often that first step of seeing beyond the trees to the wood that is the slowest and most painful. Due to preconceived ideas of what a loving environment provides for the children within, it is much easier to overlook the problem of the abusive carer and the manipulative perpetrator who exploit the innocence of the child and the trust of the other members of the group. If we are reluctant as professionals to face up to a problem because we wish to avoid being branded racist, then we are guilty of extending and prolonging the abuse the child is subjected to. A local authority day nursery manager related a story to me about one of the children who attended a previous nursery where she was employed. The child was female, about eighteen months old and Moroccan. She witnessed the little girl inserting the handle of a push-along toy into her vagina on several occasions. The policy of the day nursery at that pre-Children Act time was that if the manager of the establishment didn't see the actual incident, then the word of the other professional could not be accepted. Some years later, she met the child and her mother again and the mother told her that the child's father had been imprisoned for child abuse. It is often the case that by the time those in authority acknowledge protective provision for a child, the damage has been done. If the training of all those working in the area of childcare includes recognition of the signs and symptoms of child abuse, and there is a satisfactory amount of anti-discriminatory awareness training carried out, perhaps, in time, more black children will be acknowledged as being in need. I will mention some of the positive professional work carried out in terms of preventive action later in the chapter. Staying with anti-discrimination for a while longer, the most disappointing aspect of this research is to discover that this is an area which appears to have gone out of fashion again. I wonder if local authorities and care establishments feel they have nothing more to offer, or that by now everyone is totally aware of the need to provide equal and appropriate provision?

> Since the 50's and 60's much has happened in Britain's race relations. In addition to the Race Relations Acts, there has been the Institute of Race Relations, Commission for Racial Equality, Community Relations Councils and a growing race relations industry. As the industry had grown, so has the 'race expertise' in various shapes and forms, ranging from race advisers/officers to specialist workers, to ethnic minority workers, section 11 workers, black and ethnic minority groups and so on.... It is not my aim to question or evaluate what quantitative or qualitative impacts the race relations industry has had in eliminating racial discrimina-

tion and inequality. Rather, I am concerned with the continuous black pain which, in spite of all these developments, cannot seek comfort in the midst of the overwhelming evidence of little change in the experiences of those black and minority ethnic families and individuals who are in need of services. Black pain which, in spite of some visible impacts, is inflicted with more pain as the impacts do not match up with the outcomes. Black pain defines these so called impacts as superficial.[3]

In this report, Bandana Ahmad goes on to say how white professionals, who somehow expect a form of gratitude for their anti-discriminatory stance, are often offended and may resort to insulting or withdrawing their services from the black ingrates. It is a difficult aspect of racism to accept, i.e. that all or most of us who assert the concept of equal rights for all may still harbour these ingrained imperialistic tendencies. The problem is that these tendencies don't always show themselves in a manner which can be challenged. I have to stop sometimes and question my motives about certain expectations of or attitudes I have towards other people. Perhaps I am also looking for that recognition from the oppressed that I really am a fine woman despite my whiteness. How do white professionals feel when they don't receive thanks or other gestures of gratitude?

During the year it has taken for me to compile this book, I applied to attend several courses linked to racism and child abuse, or racism and the Children Act. With one exception, they were cancelled due to insufficient interest. That is the sort of racism which is the most difficult to overcome, because there are so many excuses that can be made to rationalize the absence of participants. Lack of funds, too many other pressures, 'perhaps this is just a little too specific for my needs': the list is endless. The only real fact to emerge is that we still shy away from potentially confrontational issues with regard to racist discrimination.

This becomes a double dilemma for the abused black child. If certain criteria are set which appear to redress the situation for, say, a white child, and when the same are applied to a black child with no apparent changes occurring, it would then be easy to point the finger of failure at the inability of the black child to use those facilities.

A programme designed to reduce antisocial behaviour in young children by training teachers and parents has reported mixed results, say researchers. The primary prevention programme resulted in a significant reduction in aggressive behaviour among white boys and a significant reduction in self-destructive behaviour among white girls, but the researchers report no significant differences for black subjects. The study involved 458 first grade children in eight public elementary schools in Seattle, WA, along with their parents and teachers, all of whom were assigned to experimental or control groups. The parenting curriculum, 'Catch Em Being Good', taught monitoring and supervising children's behaviour, using appropriate rewards and punishments, using consistent discipline practices, using effective communication skills, and involving children in family activities. The teachers were taught the use of proactive classroom management methods, cognitive social skills training, and interactive teaching methods. The study began in the fall of 1981, when the students entered the first grade and progress was assessed at the end of the second grade. The children were taught social skills from the Interpersonal Cognitive Problem Solving, which includes communication, decision making, negotiation and resolution skills. In addition, the teachers practiced interactive teaching, in which grades are determined by skills demonstration, not comparison. The researchers say they are encouraged by the reduction in antisocial behaviour among white students, but are troubled by the nonresponse of black students. They note, however, that 31 of the 37 teachers in the study were white and may not have been as sensitive to behaviour changes in blacks as they were to behaviour changes in whites. Another possibility, they say, is that the cognitive and affective styles of the training may be better suited to white students than black students.[4]

It is difficult to say if, as a result of this research, other methods of training would be used to assess whether the black students responded, or whether it was considered to be merely a result of their inability to change, therefore making *them* the failure, not the system.

The document *Working Together under The Children Act*[5] made several recommendations designed to assist local authorities in their efforts to support children and their families. Pre-school children were also taken into consideration. It was suggested that preventive rather than curative work be carried out with very young children who were likely to be registered as in need of protection or support. This, in some areas, resulted in the local authority day nurseries being reassessed. For example, Westminster has day nursery and family centre provision. The day nursery is used mainly by those families who need day care for their young children while the parents either go to work or gain respite from the pressures of coping. The family centre is more parent/child centred. This is usually the agency which offers parents support such as counselling, advice for financial problems, etc. At the same time, parents are encouraged to take a positive look at their children's development and their role in that development. Some parents may need to learn how to play with their children. Some may need to address disciplinary issues. Although it is still too early to be really clear whether the family centre system has been successful in lowering the number of children placed on the child protection register because of the danger of sexual abuse, those workers who agreed to talk to me feel it is showing a promising effect. If parents are made to feel they are important in their child's development, some of the problems may be avoided. Some parents may need to be aware of how to protect their children from other potentially abusive adults and this may be achieved through appropriate counselling. Each local authority has taken the directives and recommendations and effected them in different ways, so it is not easy as yet to present a national comparison. The Children Act stresses the necessity of acknowledging and recognizing each child's colour, culture, ethnicity, gender, age and community. I have mentioned in previous chapters how difficult it must be for black children to feel positive about their cultural and racial background if they are withdrawn from it and placed in what amounts to an alien environment, whether or not it is for their own safety.

Perhaps this is another area which needs to be addressed. Does the child have to leave the neighbourhood? Shouldn't there be legislation which insists that appropriate accommodation and care be provided for black children, or as near as possible to their familiar environment? This doesn't need to cost a fortune. Just as there were readjustments carried out with existing facilities to enable parents to hone the skills they had, and for pre-school children to be given additional protection and nurturing, the same could be done with existing residential care establishments. They could be made multicultural in terms of the children residing there and the staff who work there, or, within each local authority, a residential setting could be established which is more appropriate to ethnic minority children than to white children. It should be the duty of every local authority to ensure that black children in particular do not become alienated from their peers and their community.

In her paper, *Looking for Linda*, Barbara Williams[6] highlights the plight of a black girl placed in the care of a local authority in America. She is treated as a white child with black skin and responds as a white child, cancelling out any of the behaviours or language that emphasize her colour. She is surrounded by white role models and when she does step out of line – by experimenting with drugs as do lots of white and black youngsters – she is sent to a detention centre while her white friends are given either a warning or probation. Even at the centre Linda does well, as the officers are again mainly white. In short, Linda loses her black identity and when her dreams reflect this by emphasizing a longing to be white, to belong, the caseworker realizes the extent of the problems for her.

> Most of the time, professional social work has self-consciously tried to be colourblind in dealing with children of minority groups. This may ease the conscience, but the unconscious biases and the mores of the system make themselves felt. Stechno (1982) points out that the differences in the placement and treatment of minority youths and white youths by social services systems are still clearly visible, with black children underrepresented in the most sophisticated treatment facilities, such as group homes and residential treatment centers. Even when these children do make it to these settings, any lack of cultural awareness and understanding may well work to their detriment. Turning a blind eye to color and pretending that it does not exist denies core identity in any person. Simply 'changing' the orientation of a child, though it may be satisfying to the worker and apparently successful, cannot be anything but harmful in the end.[7]

Where a black child has a language of origin which is not English, the difficulty for the parents in particular is compounded. It would be impossible to employ interpreters for each language a family may speak, as there are so many. But if a situation arises where the seriousness of it means intervention and support from the statutory bodies, then every effort must be made to find a suitable person. This is where the leaders of local communities can play a part. Increased liaison with various groups is necessary and can only provide positive action in the long term. The training of interpreters in aspects of child abuse and anti-discriminatory practice is essential. I had occasion to work with a relative of a deaf child abuse survivor. The trauma of the abuse was aggravated for her by the person who was brought in to assist her through her statement by using sign language. The signer was so biased and insensitive to the child's difficulties that initially she didn't give the correct information to the police, and she spent some of the supposed interpretation time admonishing the child for being dirty and naughty. It was only when the child told her mother that the situation was resolved and the translator sacked. We cannot assume that all translators are without prejudice.

As professional carers in whatever field are recruited, there should be a much more active drive towards selection of those candidates who reflect the community cultures. It is pointless employing, for example, a white social worker in a predominantly black area if all the other team members are also white or from other culturally distant groups. However aware that worker might be, he or she cannot make up for the lack of historical similarity. Many people would say, but if that person was the best at interview, then it is not practising equality of opportunity if he or she is not offered the post. My response is that professionals are employed to give a service to the community. If no suitable black workers apply, the question must be, what needs to be done to encourage them? It cannot be assumed that the best black people have applied for the job. There is a danger, however, that assumptions are made about the awareness of all black professionals of cultures other than those they were born into. All workers should go through cultural awareness training. An inappropriate attitude from a black professional towards a black family from a different background may cause more damaging alienation for the family, who will now feel they have no one who understands. Black professionals can be as fixed in their prejudice as white professionals. In a mixed black cultural group, each person might have a different history, a different religion, a different expectation and a different perspective of their role, their rights and their status.

The final words of this book must, of course, be dedicated to the children it is designed to support. I would like to remind the reader of the devastation which child sexual abuse can wreak in the life of any child of any colour, from any culture and any language. Sexual abuse of the child is a death – the death of childhood, of innocence, of part of self. Whether that abuse began as a pleasure, even if it maintained that illusion for many years, there is still a bereavement. No one can fully enjoy the control exerted over their body and mind by another. Black children have many of their natural rights and privileges denied them, simply because they are black. It is small wonder that many who are abused feel that there is nowhere for them to take their pain and have it understood. They have every right to be believed, supported and nurtured in the way to which they are accustomed. Too many children have been abused and too many black abused children have not been recognized. It is time to change.

Notes

1 Children Act 1989, introduction, London: HMSO, 1991.
2 F.M. Hooper, 'Significant findings in the management of child abuse in the black community of Natal and kwaZulu.' Paper presented in 1990 as an addendum to a paper presented in Brazil in 1988.
3 Bandana Ahmad, 'Black pain, white hurt'. *Social Work Today*, December 1989.
4 The Brown University Child Aggression Prevention Programme, 1991.
5 Department of Health, *Working Together under the Children Act 1989*. London: HMSO, 1991.
6 Barbara Williams, *Looking for Linda: Identity in Black and White*. Child Welfare League of America, 1987.
7 *Ibid*, p. 77.

APPENDIX
Abuse Survey

(Please answer the questions as fully as you can.)

1 State whether you are male/female.

2 Circle the age range that applies to you at present: 15/20
   20/25   25/30   30/35   35/40   40/45   45/50

3 Circle the age range you were when the abuse began: 1/5   5/10
   10/15   15/20

4 Circle the cultural and/or religious group you feel best describes
   you: Caribbean African   Asian   Mixed culture (please state
   which cultures)   Christian   Muslim Hindu   Other (please
   state)

5 i   Was your abuser: a) a family member   b) a family friend
      c) a member of your community, e.g. teacher, priest, etc.
      d) a stranger   e) other (please state)_____

  ii   Was your abuser from the same cultural group?

      If 'no', what group did they belong to?

6 Was your abuser(s) male or female? (If there has been more than
   one abuser, please state the gender of each one.)

7 Circle the approximate age of your abuser when the abuse began:
   15/20   20/25   25/30   30/35   35/40   40/45   45/50
   50/55   55/60   older

8 How long did the abuse continue?

9 Has the abuse now stopped?

10 How did the abuse stop?

   Did you tell? (If 'Yes' please answer all the questions in section
   10. If 'no' please go on to question 11.)

   i   Whom did you tell?

   ii   Did they believe you?

   iii What did they do?

   iv   Did the abuse stop?

        If 'no', how did it eventually stop?

        Please answer as fully as possible.

11 Answer these questions if your answer to question 10 was 'no'.

   i   How did the abuse stop?

ii Did you tell? (If 'no' please answer the following questions in this section.)

iii Did you keep quiet because you thought no one would believe you?

iv Did your abuser threaten you in some way? Please explain how.

v Did you feel that in some way, people would assume that this sort of thing was common in your culture and that if you told, you would be betraying that culture?

(Any feelings you wish to write here would be welcome.)

12 Were you able to eventually leave the abusive situation?

(If 'yes' please continue to answer the questions in this section. If 'no' please go to question 13.)

i Where did you go?

ii How old were you?

iii Do you still have any contact with your abuser?

(Any thoughts or feelings you may wish to include here would be welcome.)

13 Did the abuser eventually leave?

14   Has the abuse stopped now?

     If 'no' what help or support are you seeking?

15   Were the police or social services involved in this situation at any time?

     What happened?

     (Please write as full an account as you feel you are able.)

16   Did you receive any support from a social worker or counsellor from your own cultural background?

     If 'yes' please describe the type of support and its effectiveness.

     Are you still receiving support?

17   Did you at any time consider that this happened to you because you were bad?

18   Did you at any time consider that this happened to you because you belonged to a particular cultural group?

19   Did you at any time consider that this happened to you because you were a particular gender?

20   Do you feel, in general, that abuse of children from non-white cultures gets passed over as being unimportant?

21 Have you anything else you wish to say, either about questions that were not asked, or further information you feel would be important to me in my research?

INDEX

abuse 21
abusers 22, 23
Africans 2, 4, 8, 35, 65
arranged marriage 71

Bandana, Ahmad 74
Beckett, J.O. 66
black, definition 2
black pain 74
black professional 27, 30
black skin 9, 15, 22
blame 70
Borrowdale, Ann 13, 20
Bulger, James 25

Caribbean 28, 29, 31, 34, 36, 37
case conference 41
case studies 28–39
   Leon 43–53
   Sunita 53–62
Catholic Church 19
Child Protection Register 64, 65
ChildLine 67
Children Act (1989) vi, vii, 6, 7, 13,
   24, 42, 52, 64, 75, 76
circumcision
   female 16
   male 16, 17
Coley, S.M. 66
'colour-blind approach' 8
cultural background 7
culture
   definition 3, 27
   distant 78

Darwin, Charles 3
Droisen, Audrey 7
Dworkin, Andrea 8, 22

Eid 62
ethnicity 3
evidence 63

Finklehor, David 67
footbinding 17

Hampton, R.I. 66
Hooper, F.M. 72
Hoover, J. Edgar 5
Huff, Darrell 63
Hume, David 3

identity 6
incest vii, 12, 14
interpreters 27, 78

keeping safe 23, 24
kissing 23

languages 9
loyalty 66
Lyons, Drw Christina 24

Madras 23
Miles, Rosalind 25
minorities 3, 5
mothers 12, 13, 14
Mrazek, P.J. 67
Muslim 5, 6, 20, 53, 65
myths 11, 14, 17

nationalism 3
NSPCC 67
Newham, London Borough of 65

Race Relations Acts 73
racism 3

Ramadan 53
rape 13, 18, 20
revenge 12
Roberts, Catherine 23
Russell, Diana 65, 67

self-image 4, 7, 8, 9, 24, 70
slavery 14
Southall Black Women's Centre 66
Stoller, Robert 8

tradition vii, 14, 16, 32

victim 22

West, Fred 14
West, Rosemary 14
Westminster, London Borough of, 75
Williams, Barbara 77
Wyatt, Gail 65, 67

Yawar, Tasnim 5, 6

Zulu community, Natal 72